Shakespeare

&

the Tudor Rose

Shakespeare

&

the Tudor Rose

Elisabeth Sears

Meadow Geese Press
Marshfield Hills
Massachusetts

Meadow Geese Press
Box 345, Marshfield Hills, Massachusetts 02051

© 2002 Elisabeth Sears
All Rights Reserved

First Edition, First Printing
April, 2003

ISBN: 0-9665564-4-5
Library of Congress Control Number: 2002102931

Printed in the United States of America

To my children and their spouses
Clara and Skip Knapp, Mary Bang,
Esther and Roy Loman, Katharine and Joe Wood,
Joseph Laderoute Jr., Paul and Sarah Laderoute,
Evelyn and Kent Belden

and
my grandchildren
Heather Knapp Livingston & Mitchell Livingston,
Katharine Knapp, Megan Bang, Peter Bang, Sarah Loman,
Daniel Loman, David Loman, Morgan Wood, Kyle Wood,
Joseph Laderoute III, Shane Laderoute, Bennett Laderoute,
Carson Laderoute, Andrew Laderoute,
Justin Belden, Carling Belden

and
my great-grandson
Ryan Mitchell Livingston

Contents

Acknowledgments

My parents, Edmund H. and Sophia Whitney Sears, gave me every chance to be an educated, contributing citizen, but must have felt they had failed. Now, late in life, I fully appreciate all they did for me. My own children have made me proud of their accomplishments. Would that I had done as much for my parents.

My sixteen wonderful grandchildren mean more to me than I could have ever imagined. My oldest grandchild, Heather Knapp Livingston, has given me my first great-grandson, Ryan. All these family members have had immense influences on me and have been consistently supportive of my obsession for discovering the truth about 'Shakespeare'. My son-in-law, Skip Knapp, not only critiques my writing, but helps me in my ongoing struggle with computer snags.

Two professors in college influenced me. Dr. Robert Aborn was teacher and advisor for my music major. Dr. Theodore Steele, my mentor for my English major, gave me a memorable introduction to Shakespeare. It was in his Shakespeare class that the Sonnets first really affected me, so much so that I wrote an extra paper about the *Dynastic tone* of the Sonnets! Then, graduate school at Bread Loaf, Middlebury, changed my life completely in three years of study in Renaissance Literature and philosophy with Dr. A. Bartlett Giamatti. To these professors I am tremendously indebted, but Bart Giamatti, his brilliant teaching, his kindness, his character, changed my life forevermore.

My children and grandchildren have been tolerant of my thirty-year Oxfordian quest, and have provided great moral support. My daughter, Clara Knapp, helped me search ancient records in England and was present when the second earl of Southhampton's will was put in my hands at the Winchester Ancient Records Office. This document set me on the trail of innumerable non sequiturs in Tudor History.

More than ten years ago, a longtime friend, Tom Winship, took time in his busy life as managing editor of the Boston Globe to look at my 500-page rough manuscript and solved my problem of how to proceed. Tom, with a telephone call to Herb Kenney, editorial writer for the Globe, set me up for an interview. Two days later, my meeting with Herb proved to be exactly right. There was no time wasted explaining who the earl of Oxford was. Herb, a classmate of Charlton Ogburn's at Harvard, was then currently editing each chapter of Charlton's book, *The Mysterious William Shakespeare*, an incredible coincidence that Tom knew nothing about when he recommended Herb. Under Herb's guidance, the original *Shakespeare and the Tudor Rose* was rewritten three times, and, in the process, slimmed down considerably, before this wonderful taskmaster said, "Go with it."

My everlasting gratitude goes to Hank Whittemore for his kind words and loyal support in his introduction to this edition. From such a brilliant author and someone whom I admire immensely, this is appreciated more than I can express. Hank also took time from writing his own book to search for vitally important records needed for *Shakespeare and the Tudor Rose*.

Finally, and far from the least, I give heartfelt thanks to my brilliant and exacting publisher, Steve Aucella, who has taught me so much along the way, not just about publishing, but about human nature and how to live his motto: *Press on Regardless!*

Elisabeth Sears
March 28, 2002

Cover portrait by
kind permission of
His Grace
the Duke of Buccleuch and
Queensbury, K.T.

Introduction

THIS BOOK is a brilliant achievement, a landmark in the effort to understand the mysteries of William Shakespeare. Let us note Elisabeth Sears is first among us to perceive, through the dim haze of history as recorded, how events come together to form a clear pattern of cause and effect that has eluded us for centuries. A book like this one — and such books are rare indeed — necessarily draws its share of criticism, but the prediction here is that the critics will eventually accept this clear pattern and the heretofore untold story it reveals, in terms of its fundamental grasp of the truth. Regardless of our different views of the particulars, here, folks, is what really happened.

Even for the growing numbers of students who have come to realize that Edward de Vere, seventeenth earl of Oxford (1550-1604), was the author of the poems and plays attributed to William Shakespeare, there remains scant recognition this story is not simply a literary one. Behind it is a human drama inextricable from the politics of the Elizabethan Age. As this tale unfolds in the capable hands of Betty Sears, we perceive a powerful irony early on: if the traditional tale of Shakespeare has been a myth, then some legend of at least equal potency must have been lurking right behind it all along.

This legend is that of Elizabeth I of England as the Virgin Queen. The big lie of history that gave rise to the big lie of

"William Shakespeare" was, after all, the myth that this remarkable monarch remained childless and therefore left no issue of her body to succeed her. The hidden story behind the hidden author is that, when the Queen died on March 24, 1603, bringing her Tudor Rose dynasty to its end, in fact she did have a royal son who deserved to inherit the throne.

Lord Edward de Vere of Oxford told this truth in his magnificent writings, preserving it for posterity, and in the process took it upon himself to bury his own authorship under the pen name that has so gloriously survived and endured. It was Oxford's own beloved son by Queen Elizabeth herself, the great nobleman Henry Wriothesley, third earl of Southampton, who should have succeeded his mother as Henry IX of England. And it was this same younger earl to whom his father in the Sonnets summed up the story in just two lines of Sonnet 81:

> Your name from hence immortal life shall have,
> Though I, once gone, to all the world must die.

As this book demonstrates, the story behind "Shakespeare" is inseparable from that of the royal succession. The real events in the life of the author, echoing his own chronicle plays of English history, involve the ever-growing power struggle around Elizabeth's throne in the latter years of her reign.

What history has recorded is how the Queen's chief minister William Cecil, Lord Burghley, and then his own son, Robert Cecil, managed to check the wild ambitions of Robert Devereux, second earl of Essex, whose attempt to remove the Cecilian stranglehold culminated in the Rebellion of February 8, 1601. But now Ms. Sears fills in what we had failed to understand about this tragic episode, which resulted in the execution of

Essex and the confinement of Southampton in the Tower of London for more than two years. What we hadn't known was that the Queen's own son languished in prison at the time of her death, when James VI of Scotland succeeded her as James I of England, and that meanwhile his father, the earl of Oxford, was desperately trying to save him.

In return for Southampton's freedom, his claim by blood to the throne had to be sacrificed. And because Edward de Vere had revealed this claim in his writings, especially within the Sonnets, he was forced to deny not only his fatherhood but also his responsibility for having created the single greatest outpouring of literature the world has ever known.

"My name be buried where my body is," Edward de Vere cried out in Sonnet 72, knowing he was preserving the truth for future generations.

"'Gainst death and all oblivious enmity shall you pace forth," he told his royal son in Sonnet 55, adding, "Your praise shall still find room even in the eyes of all posterity that wear this world out to the ending doom."

It's thrilling beyond words watching Henry Wriothesley, heir of the Tudor Rose, at long last "pace forth" in these pages.

Elisabeth Sears has built upon the shoulders of J. Thomas Looney in 1920, Charlton and Dorothy Ogburn in 1952, and Charlton Ogburn Jr. in 1984. She has also given us something new and essential. Here is that clear pattern of events, that all-important historical and political context, within which the "authorship mystery" finally makes sense. She also now leads the way in resurrecting the man who was William Shakespeare.

Hank Whittemore, Upper Nyack, NY
May, 2001

1 🌼 SUMMER'S WELCOME

QUEEN ELIZABETH established the custom early in her reign of making an annual Royal Progress through the countryside to show herself to her people. Her graciousness to her subjects on public occasions made her perhaps the most popular monarch who had ever ruled England. Addressing her Privy Council and thirty members of the House of Commons on February 6, 1559, Elizabeth insisted that the people of Britain were her family, that she did not need a husband, and that she was wedded to her Kingdom.

> Now that the public care of governing the Kingdom is laid upon me, to draw upon me also the cares of marriage, may seem a point of inconsiderate Folly. Yes, to satisfy you, I have joined myself in Marriage to an Husband, namely, the Kingdom of England. And behold, which marvel you have forgotten, the pledge of this (her coronation ring) my Wedlock and Marriage with my Kingdom.[1]

Thus, the annual summer progress of the Queen was critically important as a means of maintaining her rapport with her family, the people of England. Year after year her cumbersome caravan wound through the countryside, staying several days at a time at the manor houses of her courtiers, an honor for them, but devastatingly costly as well.

Nichols' *Progresses of Queen Elizabeth* tells us that the Queen retired to Havering before going on progress to Bristow (Bristol) in 1574. Havering atte Bowre on the Thames was a thousand-acre estate, owned by the Vere's in ancient times, which later had become the property of the Crown. Elizabeth had spent some of her happiest days there as a four-year old, when it was the Royal Nursery for her baby brother, Prince Edward. For Elizabeth, it had warm childhood memories of the little brother she loved dearly. It was a time, too, when Elizabeth was first treated with loving kindness by her new governess, Kat Ashley. Thus Havering was a place of happy memories and always a safe haven for the Queen.

From Havering, Elizabeth proceeded on to Bristol and there is a report that the Queen may have gone from 'Bristow' into Wales, remaining there for a week or so. But, from the end of May to the beginning of July, there are no records of Queen Elizabeth's activities, and it seems likely that a child was born sometime between the end of May and the beginning of July.

There had been much talk in 1572 that the earl of Oxford was the Queen's favorite and he seemed to remain in high favor until July of 1574. Then, Edward de Vere suddenly fled, with young Edward Seymour, to the Continent. The Queen sent two of her Gentlemen Pensioners to bring them home and the crisis seemed to be resolved. Since it was treason to leave the country without the Queen's License, Oxford must have had a cogent reason for his sudden flight from England.

Much of the information of these mysterious happenings is recorded in the Shakespeare Sonnets and plays. Sonnet 56 seems to refer to the Queen's melancholy in these weeks of wanderings followed by a return to Havering, the Queen's favorite spot, at the end of May:

> ...do not kill
> The spirit of love with a perpetual dullness.

This sonnet also speaks of the location on the water at the lower reaches of the Thames:

> Which parts the shore where two contracted new
> Come daily to the banks...

It also stresses that it is a time of waiting for an event expected in the summer: "Makes summer's welcome thrice more wish'd, more rare." According to Dorothy and Charlton Ogburn, Sr, Oxford accompanied the Queen in February, 1574 on a visit to Archbishop Parker in Canterbury. The Ogburns felt that the Queen and Oxford plighted their troth at that time.[2] Also, a collection of poems titled, *A Hundred Sundrie Flowres,* published under the posy, Meritum Petere Grave, included a narrative poem, *Dan Bartholomew of Bathe,* signed Fata non Fortuna , which was the final selection in the volume. When the earl of Oxford was traveling in Italy in 1575 and 1576, this same collection was republished as *The Posies of George Gascoigne.*[3] Proponents of Oxford-as-Shakespeare are convinced that Oxford was the author hidden by the two poesies, Meritum Petere Grave and Fata Non Fortuna. Therefore, when Dan Bartholomew complains that Ferenda Natura (Cruel nature) first wooed and won him (and when he had her by "faith and troth assured"), but then afterwards proved false, it is Oxford's bitter complaint about Queen Elizabeth. The poem begins, however, with the earlier romance and includes those lines that tell us of their betrothal, a formal ceremony, which was then almost as binding as a marriage rite.

The reference in Sonnet 56 to the "shore" and the half-line, "Come daily to the banks" echoes Titania's description in *A Midsummer Night's Dream*. "Summer's welcome" has a double sense. It alludes to the arrival of summer in June and to the welcoming of a son (perhaps on Midsummer Night).

Much of the plot of *A Midsummer Night's Dream* revolves around Oberon and Titania's dispute over a little changeling child. In Act II, scene 1, Titania (an Ovidian variant of Diana), queen of the fairies, meeting Oberon in the forest, spurns his pleadings for the little changeling child.

Oberon: I do but beg a little changeling boy
      To be my henchman.
Queen: Set your heart at rest
      The *fairyland* buys not the child of me.*
      His mother was a *vot'ress* of my order
      -
      And sat with me on Neptune's yellow sands,
      Marking th' embarked traders on the flood;
      When we have laugh'd to see the sails conceive
      And grow big-bellied with the wanton wind;
      Which she with pretty and with swimming gait
      Following (*her womb then rich with my young squire*)
      Would imitate, and sail upon the land
      To fetch me trifles, and return again,
      As from a voyage, rich with merchandise.

* —"child of me" as in "child of my body".

Fairyland seems to represent "Vere-y land", much as the *Fair Youth* of the Sonnets seems to stand for the *Vere Youth*, and the *Vot'ress* refers to Queen Elizabeth. "The embarked traders on the flood" depicts the scene on the lower reaches of the Thames that Elizabeth and Oxford would have observed at Havering. The description of the *vot'ress* must then be seen as a charming depiction of the Queen just prior to the birth of the child.

A Midsummer Night's Dream offers still more suggestions of the Elizabeth-Oxford relationship. In Act II, scene 1, the following speech by Oberon also seems to echo the situation at Havering in 1574:

> Oberon: --Cupid, all arm'd. A certain aim he took
> At a **fair Vestral, throned by the West**,
> And loos'd his love shaft smartly from his bow,
> - - - - - - - - - -
> But I might see young Cupid's fiery shaft
> Quench'd in the **chaste beams of the wat'ry moon**,
> And the **imperial vot'ress** passed on,
> In **maiden meditation, fancy free**.
> - - - - - - - - - -
> It fell upon a **little Western flower**,
> Before milk-white, now **Purple** with love's wound.

"Throned by the West" is said to imply Queen Elizabeth was present, sitting on a throne or raised chair at an outdoor performance. 'By' is an odd prepositional usage. It could really refer to the throes of childbirth at the arrival of the *little Western flower,* which by its color purple denotes royalty. The moon, as usual, represents Queen Elizabeth, but there is a particular irony in the juxtaposition of *chaste beams* and *wat'ry moon*. Though the moon is known for constant change, water is even more fluid and in the guise of Proteus is known for changing from one form to another, for disguising and dissembling. The *wat'ry moon* merely pretended to be chaste. Dr. A. Bartlett Giamatti in *Play of Double Senses: Spencer's Faerie Queene* on page 89, says, "Proteus is the very principle of deceptive flux." This, then, is Oberon/Oxford's rebuke for Titania/Queen Elizabeth's duplicity. The Imperial Votress, Queen Elizabeth, seems to have passed on, in maiden meditation, fancy free by masking her child as someone else's son, a little changeling child in some-one else's household.

Sonnets 153 and 154 are not at all like the other Sonnets in the collection known as *Shakespeare's Sonnets*. Some scholars exclude them from the series, but these two have a close relationship to the foregoing exchanges in *A Midsummer Night's Dream* and tell of the initial stages of the romance between Oxford and the Queen. Though placed at the very end of the Sonnet sequence, they contain stylistic and thematic elements that identify them as the first written. They were also more derivitive in origin, having come from an ancient source, the Greek epigram by a Byzantine poet known as Marianus Scholasticus.[4]

These two sonnets refer to the tryst at Bath recorded in the long poem, *Dan Bartholomew of Bathe*. If this poem is, as so many believe, really Oxford's work, it does much to clarify the two sonnets placed deceptively at the end of the Sonnet sequence. Written in the early seventies they not only tell of the Royal romance, but stand as the work of a neophyte poet whose style and imagery would develop and mature later.

Although no exact date can be determined for the birth of

the Queen's child, it may well have been June 21, midsummer's eve, after which Oxford emerged from his dream world into harsh reality. Like Bottom, he may have said, "Methought I was. . . Methought I had. . .but man is but a patch'd fool if he will offer to say what methought I had." Only the knowledge of Oxford's experience at this time clears up the mystery of *Midsummer Night's Dream* being set in a time frame at the beginning of May, while the title places it at the summer solstice.

Evidently some disagreement arose after the birth of the child, for this is when Oxford fled to the Continent in great haste. The state papers, dated July 8, 1574, say:

> The earl of Oxford departed into Flanders without the Queen's licence, and was revoqued by the Queen sending the Ge. Pensioners for hym.[5]

Also, Ambassador Killigrew at Edinburgh notes in a letter to Sir Francis Walsingham (head of Queen Elizabeth's Secret Service) July 18, 1574:

> My Lord of Oxford and Lord Seymour are fled out of England, and passed by Bruges and Brussels.[6]

The Queen's Courtiers often found when the Queen's temper flared it was safest to absent themselves from her presence until her temper cooled. Her wrath must have been intense for Oxford to flee the country. Later, he would express not the fear that drove him from the country, but his great sorrow at his loss, in Sonnet 33:

> And from the forlorn world his visage hide,

Stealing unseen to West with this disgrace.
Even so my son one early morn did shine
With all-triumphant splendour on my brow;
But, out alack! He was but one hour mine,
The region cloud hath mask'd him from me now.

Here the sun becomes his son, who is stolen from him and hidden from the world and thus *disgraced*. The Oxford English Dictionary's definitions for 'disgraced' are: 1) to undo or mar the grace of, to deprive of outward grace; 2) to put to shame or put out of countenance by eclipsing; 3) to put out of grace or favour, to treat with disfavour, and hence with dishonour, to dismiss from (Royal, etc.) favour and honour.

Though their son is the royal heir, the Queen (Region, or Regina, Latin for Queen) has masked the child, who was Oxford's for only an hour, and he becomes a little changeling boy. 'My *sunne*', as it is spelled in the 1609 quarto (also spelled *sonne* on occasion, spelling being somewhat arbitrary in the sixteenth century), is a pun used constantly throughout the Sonnets and plays and is particularly notable in the word *sonnets*.

Oxford's initial thrill at the birth of his son and his conviction that their son would be named heir to the throne, was cruelly cut short. Elizabeth had assured herself of a Royal Tudor heir, but, "passing on in maiden meditation fancy free", avoided the open acknowledgement of the child.

Queen Elizabeth was always fearful that a consort or king would take control of her Kingdom as Philip II did with Mary Tudor's reign. Also, Elizabeth's endless marriage negotiations were the central focus of her foreign policy, which she used successfully for many years as a means of keeping the two great powers of Europe from combining forces to destroy England.

Sonnet 35 deals again with Elizabeth and Oxford's dispute, but adds more images and introduces the rose motif, so prevalent in the Fair Youth Sonnets:

Roses have thorns and silver fountains mud;
Clouds and eclipses stain both moon and sun,
And loathsome canker lives in sweetest bud.

Though one of Elizabeth's mottoes was *Rosa Sine Spina* (Rose without a thorn), Oxford seems to feel that she does have thorns after all. Oxford, represented by the 'Ver' in "Silver Fountains", admits, by adding "mud", that he has frailties, too. It may be stretching things to find a relationship between a fountain and a spring, but a spring is more apt to fill with mud than a fountain and *spring* (of the year) is *ver* in Latin. He may have used the alternate word, fountains for meter and poetic tone. It could also be a reference to the springs at Bath that he mentions in Sonnets 153 and 154.

The moon always represents the Queen, and the Sun may be the son who has been stained, or distained and disgraced, by the Queen. The loathsome canker of disgrace then lives in the sweetest bud, the infant of the Tudor Rose. It also introduces the canker rose, or eglantine, the Tudor Rose, growing wild, untended by his parents.

In Sonnet 87, Oxford renounces his rights to the child and the Queen. The legal terminology in this sonnet speaks of a solemn charter, but admits that the Queen has the power to it. This also stands as evidence of the poet's formal training as a lawyer.

The charter of thy worth gives thee releasing;

My bonds in thee are all determinate;
- --
Thus have I had thee as a dream doth flatter;
In sleep a king, but waking no such matter.

Oxford clearly understands that the Queen has the power and the right to do just as she chooses, while he must, on his allegiance, accept her and her decisions. The final couplet of Sonnet 87 echoes Bottom's bewilderment in *Midsummer Night's Dream,* when he awakes from his enchantment. Oxford, like Bottom, did indeed feel like a 'patch'd fool'. There is every indication that when the Sonnets were first published, they were intentionally not set in relation to a temporal sequence. Thus, it adds to the difficulty of understanding their meaning. Not only has this led to confusion, but there is an expression of extreme frustration and denial by the author in his complaint (Sonnet 66) that he was "tongue-tied by authority." That authority was partly the Queen, but it was also Lord Burghley. After Burghley's death in 1598, it was his son, Robert Cecil.

The Cecil's interest in Crown matters involved their political and personal advancement and was the *idée fixe* of both William and Robert Cecil. The Queen's aim was to avoid the public knowledge that she had an heir. She often expressed a fear that a known heir to the throne might stir up a faction that would depose her in favor of another heir. This, of course was exactly what happened in the case of the Catholic Mary, Queen of Scots. Queen Elizabeth lived in constant fear that one of the many Catholic plots, domestic and foreign, might succeed. Elizabeth was seemingly many times a hair's breadth from assassination, (though some plots, such as the Babington plot, have been shown as created by William Cecil, to rid himself of a rival on the Privy Council and to intimidate the Queen and make her more dependent on him).[7]

If France and Spain were to join in an attack on England, their forces could demolish the unprepared British, and Elizabeth knew well what her fate would be if that were to happen. Mary of Scotland had once also been Queen of France and she felt she had a legitimate claim to the English throne through her grandmother, Henry VIII's older sister. Philip of Spain, who married Queen Mary Tudor, felt that he, by right of his marriage, was still King of England. Thus, Elizabeth had reason to worry about her safety.

By the 1580s, King Phillip had retired to the Escorial, his magnificent hilltop retreat, where he lived a hermit's life in a small cell next to the chapel. Though Elizabeth and her Privy Council seemed unaware of it, Philip, in his retirement, was reluctant to attack Britain. The Pope, however, finally persuaded Philip of his duty to the Church and to the Pope to reclaim England from the heretics. It was only then that he began preparing for the "Great Enterprise" against the 'helpless' little island Kingdom. By then, Philip had no intention of returning to England himself, but on the almost clear certainty that his mighty Armada would defeat England's inferior naval and land defences, he determined to give the realm to his daughter after conquering the English.[8]

Therefore, it was not just the Queen's personal image as the Virgin Queen that was at stake, but it was also the international political situation and Elizabeth's precarious perch on the throne of England. For years, in spite of a vast age difference, she used marriage negotiations with Le Duc d'Alençon to disrupt relations between France and Spain. Though he was in his teens and Elizabeth in her late thirties when the match was first proposed, the French took her seriously. This game was played successfully until Elizabeth was fifty-four years old. Though there were rumors that the Queen had an heir, they were not taken seriously. Had they really believed she had an heir, the combined forces of France and Spain might have attacked England many years earlier, when Philip was directly involved in worldly affairs and the English powerless to defend themselves. It was necessary for Oxford to be tongue-tied by authority then, and later events would make it even more imperative that this state secret be maintained forever. Until recently, therefore, the Sonnets have remained a mystery and Elizabeth devised in 1574 an almost perfect scheme to mask, or disguise, her son. Her choice of surrogate parents, the second earl and countess of Southampton, seemed, at the time, a perfect solution.

Southampton, one of the Queen's devout Catholic subjects, had been in trouble with the state for several years due to his divided loyalties between the Pope's edicts and his duty to the Queen. First, he was apprehended seeking advice from a Jesuit in a rendezvous in the marshes. Then later, being implicated in the Ridolfi plot to overthrow Elizabeth, he was tried for treason and condemned to death. However, after languishing in prison for some months, his sentence was commuted and in May of 1573 he was given limited freedom in the custody of Sir William More of Losely.

A few months later he was allowed to join his wife at his father-in-law's estate at Cowdrey, a short distance from Losely. On October 6, 1573 his wife bore him a son. A letter from the second earl of Southampton to Sir William More reports the birth and invites Lady More to visit the countess and their son. There the account ends. Though there is no record of this child's death, it has been reported that Henry Wriothesly was the second son. Charlotte Stopes, British historian and biographer of the third earl of Southampton, searched the available records carefully, but could not solve the mystery of the rumor that there were two sons.

Mrs. Stopes' stated purpose in researching Southampton was to clear up the blank spots in the life of Shakespeare, but she was unable to find any contact whatsoever between William Shaksper of Stratford-on-Avon and Henry Wriothesley. Mrs. Stopes felt she had failed miserably, by finding absolutely no connection between Shakespeare and his supposed sponsor, Southampton, but was perplexed by the rumor that there was a second son. This latter she discarded simply as a rumor of no consequence, yet she includes several letters from the widowed second countess of Southampton to her influential cousin, the earl of Leicester, begging him to intercede with the Queen to have the child cared for by its own kin.[9] Thus, Charlottte Stopes missed the most important 'Shakespeare' clue, that this child was the little changeling of *Midsummer Night's Dream*. And Regina's cloud has masked the Royal Prince for over 400 years.

Elizabeth probably used the threat of the executioner's block to persuade the second earl of Southampton to give the little changeling a home. It must have been heartbreaking to deny his own son his heritage and a fearful responsibility to have charge of the Queen's son.

At this time, there was a curious addition to the Southampton household. The earl acquired a gentleman of the bed chamber, Thomas Dymoke, listed in Burke's Landed Gentry as "Thomas Dymoke of Grays Inn".

Thomas Dymoke had a curious connection to Queen Elizabeth through Henry VIII and Bessie Blount's illegitimate son, the duke of Richmond. Richmond had been created duke and made heir to the throne at six years old when it seemed obvious that Queen Katherine was unable to produce a male heir. Later, the beautiful Elizabeth Blount married the earl of Lincoln and had a daughter, Bridget. Bridget married Sir Robert Dymoke, who was Thomas Dymoke's great uncle. Thus Robert Dymoke was a brother-in-law of the duke of Richmond who was half brother of Queen Elizabeth. Thomas Dymoke was also the great grandson of Sir Edward Dymoke, Queen Elizabeth's official Champion at her coronation.[10]

Thus, this lawyer from Grays Inn, with close ties to Queen Elizabeth, was put in charge of the Southampton family. Thomas Dymoke eventually returned to London and a distinguished career at Grays Inn, but for several years he was established in the Southampton household as a servant of the bed-chamber. During his time of service at Tichfield, he proved to be the cause of much distress and anguish for the second earl of Southampton and his countess.

2 ⅋ FAIR FRIEND

SOON AFTER HIS RETURN home to Tichfield in 1575 with the infant Henry and the Queen's special agent, Thomas Dymoke, the second earl of Southampton was awarded several small offices. As prudent and parsimonious as she was about grants and honors, the Queen must have felt obliged to give her son's surrogate parent some reward for his services. In 1574 he was appointed to the Commission of the Peace for Hampshire. Then in 1579 he served on a special commission for the suppression of piracy. Although his financial lot was improved by these favors, other stresses began to appear.

By 1577 the earl's wife was allegedly creating trouble. According to one account:

> ". . . the earl, upset at the intimacy of her friendship with a
> man named Donsame, 'a common person,' forbade her ever
> to see him again."[1]

If Donsame was the man given the charge of caring for her real son, the Countess may have secretly made many trips to Donsame's home in Dogmersfield to visit her little boy. It seems that this first warning was not sufficient to restrain the instincts of a mother, for in 1580 she was caught once more on a visit to

Dogmersfield. This time "in a fury, the Earl broke with his wife completely."[2]

Perhaps the earl's fury was based on fear or perhaps it was merely dictated by Dymoke. Whatever the earl's actual feelings may have been, his wife was removed from Tichfield and sent to one of the earl's secluded Hampshire residences, where she was kept under close surveillance. The earl also made (or was forced by Dymoke to make) a complete break with his wife's family, Lord and Lady Montague of Cowdrey. As it was with the Montagues and Capulets, so it was with the Montagues and the Southamptons; even the servants took up the family quarrel:

> This day Edmund Prety, Servant to the Earl of Southampton was for certain misdemeanors by him used against Mr. Anthony Brown, the eldest son of the Lord Montague . . . committed to the Marshalsea.[3]

The countess of Southampton, in a letter written to her father March 21, 1580, gives this account of the dispute. Akrigg observes that the earl was apparently dealing with the countess "only through an intermediary, one Thomas Dymoke, a gentleman of his bedchamber, and notes that the Countess is vehement against Dymoke."

> (Dymoke) is the begynner and contynnuer of the dissention betwene us...this howse is not for them that will not honor Dymoke as a god. The Earl himself so doubtful and perplexed betwene hate and dread, as what to do he knoweth nott well.[4]

The countess continues railing at the injustice of the charges against her and continues to protest her innocence in a lengthy letter:

> ...and then I should be acquited of greater evell, than overmuch folly, for desireinge or doinge that, which, being by my enemyes mistaken, doth brede this my slander and danger.[5]

Dymoke had told the countess that the earl would be reconciled with her only if the Queen herself "instructs him to end their separation, and that she would never do, for Her Majesty would never open her mouth on his wife's behalf."[6] Therefore, the countess concludes with a plea that Lord Montague ask the Privy Council to give a secret hearing of her case. This was obviously no private domestic difficulty that required the intervention of the Queen and the Privy Council, but an affair of State relating to the heir to the throne. Dymoke not only received his orders from the Queen but also acted only in her interests. The private sufferings of the Southamptons were secondary to the safeguarding of the Queen's secret. The countess, with a fond mother's desire to see her own son, could not be allowed to jeopardize the anonymity of the Royal Heir.

Thomas Dymoke was creating other hardships for the Southamptons. In his disguise as "gentleman of the bedchamber" he conveyed messages to the earl from the Jesuit martyr, Edmund Campion (who was subsequently hanged, drawn and quartered). This illicit communication was reported to authorities in London (undoubtedly by Dymoke) upon which the earl was again arrested and imprisoned in August of 1581. He was soon released and allowed to return to Tichfield, but he died on October 4, 1581. Whether he died of natural causes or, having proved to be a troublesome surrogate parent, was quietly 'disposed of' by the Queen's agent, history does not record. The third earl of Southampton, then a seven-year-old, became a ward of the Crown (ironically, a ward of his own mother) and spent the rest of his minority in the home of William Cecil, Lord Burghley.

Three months before he died, the second earl had drawn up a will with the aid of his resident lawyer-gentleman of the bedchamber. In the will he left orders for his executors to erect an elaborate tomb with effigies of himself and his parents, as well as a statue of the third earl kneeling in a mourning pose. Although the second earl had suffered much personal anguish in nurturing Elizabeth's son, he must have felt a degree of pride, too, in the honor of caring for the next Tudor monarch. Perhaps he felt that the statue of the kneeling boy would be a visible reminder that he had served his Sovereign well, in spite of his conviction for treason.

The executors of the earl's will were listed as Charles Paget, Edward Gage of Bentley in Sussex, Gilbert Wells, Ralph Hare, and Thomas Dymoke. The earl of Northumberland, Lord Paget, and a brother-in-law, Thomas Cornwallis, were designated as "overseers" to guarantee that the executors carried out the instructions of the will.[7]

Not only was Dymoke named as one of the five executors, but either with Charles Paget, or alone if necessary, he was to rule on the interpretation of any disputed clause in the will. Akrigg points out in his biography of the third earl:

> The benefits for Dymoke are many and praise of him abounds. He is allotted a special legacy of £200 (Because of the 'good opynion and faithfull trust' that the Earl has

in him, he stipulated that Dymoke is 'to be attendant and dayly about the person of my sonn'). For this Dymock is to receive another £40 a year. Until the Third Earl is of age, Dymoke is to have Whitley House for his own residence. He is authorized to keep stock in Whitley Park and in the great park at Tichfield and he is to be supplied with hay and fuel.[8]

The benefits for Dymoke go on and on: a twenty-one year lease on another farm and the earl's best horse. Dymoke, in drawing up the will, saw that he, himself, was well served. Southampton evidently could do nothing but comply. How it must have grieved him to give so much to the Queen's agent, whom he hated and feared.

However, at some time before he died, the earl found an opportunity to add a codicil to his will, presumably without the knowledge of Dymoke, that gave his wife an annuity of £80 and a bequest of £500. He also managed to include a small bequest for Lord Montague "in token of perfect love and charity between us." This last certainly indicates that his personal feelings were at odds with the sentiments dictated by Dymoke earlier.

One clause that the earl managed to add to his will is of particular note. It provides for the education until the age of twenty-one of "William, my Beggar boye." He could do no more for his own son without revealing the royal secret. William was probably named for Sir William More, who had been the second earl's warder after his release from the Tower. They had become fast friends during the earl's stay with More at Losely. When the Wriothesley boy was born in October of 1573, the first announcement of the birth went immediately to Sir William More. It was natural for Southampton to show his appreciation for the kindness shown him while he was at Losely to name his first son for his good friend and warder, Sir William More.

After the second earl's death, the widowed countess, outraged by Dymoke's arrangements, set out to cancel the earl's will. Her family had important connections, most notably the earl of Leicester. To him the countess wrote a strong letter in which she castigated Dymoke and pleaded with Leicester to use his influence to nullify Southampton's will. Though Leicester did not write a direct reply to the Countess, he did send one to her father, Lord Montague.

Leicester evidently was able to accomplish much for the countess. First, she regained custody of her daughter, Mary, which had been withheld from her under the terms of Dymoke's version of the will. Next, a compromise was worked out with Dymoke giving him the benefits allowed in the will but removing him from the administration of the estate, which was then turned over to Edward Gage.

On June 13, 1582 an "inquisition post mortem" took place in Hampshire for the disposition of the Southampton estate. The countess was allowed about one third of the earl's properties, including Dogmersfield, under the terms of her marriage settlement. Since the late earl had owned numerous manors, farms and estates, the countess' share was ample for her well-being and security.

The Queen was allowed another third of the properties during the third earl's minority, administered by the purchaser of the child's wardship. This wardship was taken over by the Master of Wards, William Cecil, on behalf of the Crown, and sold to the highest bidder. The third part of the estate, though left for the use of the minor heir, was also administered by the purchaser of the wardship and theoretically used for the needs of the child. While this was the practice in theory, in reality a wealthy estate was often exploited much to the advantage of the guardian. This was actually the lucrative business by which William Cecil enlarged his own estate enormously. Another aspect of the wardship was the right of the guardian to arrange the marriage of his ward. If the ward refused to marry as ordered, he was required to pay a large fine. If he agreed to marry the chosen bride, the guardian received a dowry from the girl's parents. Thus, the benefits of wardship were almost unlimited.

The wardship of the young earl of Southampton was "solde to the Right Honorable Charles, Lord Howard of Effingham, Lord Chamberlain to her Majestye, for one thousand pounds."[9]

> However, though Lord Howard officially purchased the wardship and though it was duly assigned at the inquisition, some further arrangements were made, *documentation of which is lacking, by which William Cecil, Lord Burghley, Master of the wards, ended up with the custody and charge of the young Earl*, while Howard continued to administer his lands. [10]

Although there is no further report of "William, my beggar boye," Edward Gage, as the chief executor of the second earl's will, may have undertaken responsibility for his education. Whatever happened to William is not otherwise recorded, but in 1582 the seven-year-old Henry, with his wardship somehow re-assigned to Lord Burghley, was introduced to a new life at Cecil House in London on the north side of the Strand. While living there, the young earl would suffer from the self-serving, greed, and viciousness of Lord Burghley, much as his real father, Oxford, had before him. Though Oxford may have worried about the future of his son in the hands of Burghley, he must have felt that Southampton, the Royal Heir, would not be as vulnerable as he himself had been to the depredations of that insatiable cormorant, the Master of the Wards. Surely the Queen would have some control over her son's welfare.

Southampton's presence at Cecil House gave Oxford the opportunity to see his royal son in London. Though Oxford had truly loved Elizabeth and for a while was enamored of Anne Vavasour, it was the paternal love for his handsome first-born and royal son that was the most compelling force in his life. The sonnets inspired by Southampton were outpourings of love, fealty and hope for the future. Any parent who has adored a promising child should instantly recognize the parental love expressed in these sonnets.

Sonnets 104 and 105 both represent this attitude of devotion to a beloved son. They also express Oxford's certainty that one day Henry would be acclaimed as the next Tudor sovereign. Sonnet 104 is typical in its tone of the doting, proud father, while Sonnet 105 shows more of Oxford's propensity for word-play on his name and title:

> To me, *fair* friend, you *never* can be old,
> For as you were when first your eye I ey'd,
> Such seems your beauty still.

Sonnet 105 is packed with word play and allusions to the Royal family:

> Let not my love be call'd idolatry

Nor my beloved as an idol show,
Since all alike my songs and praises be
To one, of one, still such, and *ever* so.

This last line includes references to Southampton's motto, *"Ung par tout et tout par ung,"* or *"All for one and one for all,"* as well as Queen Elizabeth's *"Semper Eadem"* or *"Always the Same,"* with the latter altered to "ever so" to include the third member of the family, "E. Ver."

Sonnet 105 also repeatedly stresses the three-fold family theme:

"Fair, kind and true" is all my argument,
"Fair, kind, and true," varying to other words;
And in this change is my invention spent,
Three themes in one, which wondrous scope affords.
Fair, kind, and true, have often lived alone,
Which three till now never kept seat in one.

"Fair" represents "Vere"; "Kind" is "kine," an archaic term for cattle or "Oxen"; "Kind" is also German for "child"; and "True" in Latin is "Veritas." His whole 'argument' is that Southampton is his Vere child today, tomorrow and forever. "Three themes in one" harks back to line one's denial of "idolatry." In this there is a sense of the Christian Trinity and a suggestion of the sanctity of the anointed sovereign, who is God's Vicar on earth. Though not yet crowned, Southampton was, in Oxford's eyes, the next Tudor monarch. The last line reinforces this idea, suggesting that the child is the combined essence of his parents, and in his parents' "wondrous scope," he was the great hope for their future as well as for England.

Oxford must have welcomed the turn of fate that brought Henry to Cecil House in London. but much of Oxford's joy in having his son nearby was negated by a crisis in his own life.

3 ⚜ BEGINS A JOURNEY

WHILE Southampton was growing up at Tichfield Manor, Oxford was learning the realities of Court life with its rivalries, its treacheries, and obsequies that churned about the Royal Presence. Other men sought favor, notably Christopher Hatton. He was tall, handsome, and had "danced his way into the Queen's heart with a galliard."[1] Later, Walter Ralegh would catch Elizabeth's fancy, and Robert Dudley, the earl of Leicester, was a perennial contender for the Queen's affections. Oxford found himself obliged to accept a lesser role than he had previously expected: "In sleep a king, but waking no such matter." There was a change in Oxford's view of Elizabeth after the birth of their child, a recognition that she was "unsettled still like haggard wild," who would "oft from Phoebus flee to Pan."[2] Nevertheless, though he was deeply hurt and disappointed by Elizabeth's rejection of him and their son, a closeness and a strong bond of affection remained between them to the end of their lives.

Perhaps because of this change in her relationship with Oxford and her renewed interest in Hatton, Elizabeth finally responded to Oxford's repeated requests for permission to travel abroad. Early in January of 1575 with the Queen's license granted him, Oxford left England for 16 months, traveling through France and Germany to Italy, where he stayed for almost a year.

Much of Oxford's trip to the continent is recorded in his plays, but little is reflected in his sonnets, except those addressed to Elizabeth while on his journey. In this group are Sonnets 27, 28, 43, 44, 45, 47, 48, 50, 51, 61, 113, 114. Though these demonstrate his continuing devotion to her, there is a change of tone. In these there is a certain hyperbole of flattery that replaces the genuine concern for Elizabeth before the birth of their child. There is also a contrast with the sharp reproaches in Sonnets 33, 34, and 35 that express his disillusionment in the late summer of 1574.

There was one event that occurred at this time, however, that had a harrowing effect on Oxford and left a permanent scar on his soul. What should have been a joyous occasion ultimately proved to be mortifying to his pride and damaging to his family honor.

Several years earlier, in 1571, Oxford had been betrothed to William Cecil's daughter Anne, who was then, like Juliet, just short of her fourteenth birthday. It was Cecil's right as Oxford's guardian to arrange his marriage. Though the bride was barely in her teens, Oxford at twenty-one was really beyond the age when Cecil could claim this right. It seems, too, that Cecil, as the Queen's closest adviser, must have known about Oxford's attachment to Elizabeth. The Queen may have felt that Oxford's "marriage" to Anne Cecil would silence the common gossip about her relationship with Oxford. Three years later in 1574, William Cecil undoubtedly knew that Oxford and Elizabeth had a child, a royal heir. He was deliberately sacrificing his daughter for political reasons. Yet Cecil's later manipulations of Oxford and poor Anne seem to indicate that he was doing everything possible to make their marriage valid.

In 1570 Elizabeth had begun her long series of negotiations with the French for a marriage contract, first between her and the Duc d'Anjou, and then later, and for many years, with the Duc d'Alençon. This ploy would serve her until she was fifty-four years old as a means of maintaining a balance of power with the strong Catholic factions in Europe. William Cecil was as wily as the Queen and if Oxford's and Anne's "marriage" would serve to convince the French that Elizabeth was available and serious about her negotiations, he was willing to help. Perhaps Burghley's elevation to the Peerage was his reward for the sacrifice of his daughter.

The wedding was set for September, but the groom ran away to the continent, returning only when ordered home again by the Queen. Oxford's protests were in vain. The Queen made it quite clear that Oxford must marry the girl. The wedding finally took place in the Queen's presence at Westminster Abbey in December of 1571.

The exchange between Bertram and Parolles in *All's Well That Ends Well,* in Act II, scene 3, lines 259-263, seems to reflect Oxford's own reactions in the identical circumstance of his Sovereign insisting that the young Count marry a bride against his will:

> Bertram: Although before the solemn priest I have sworn, I will not bed her.
> Parolles: What? What, sweetheart?
> Bertram: O my Parolles, they have married me! I'll to the Tuscan wars, and never bed her.

Oxford's subsequent neglect of his bride seems to verify

that Anne Cecil de Vere was perhaps his wife in name only. Ostensibly they established their residence at Wivenoe near Long Melford, one of Oxford's estates in Essex, but the earl was rarely there for he was in constant attendance on the Queen at the Court in London.

In March of 1574 Oxford accompanied the Queen on a visit to the Archbishop of Canterbury. This occasion has been identified by some as a time when Elizabeth and Oxford exchanged rings and plighted their troth.

Oxford makes the claim to Southampton "...I hallowed thy fair (Vere) name" in Sonnet 108, and it is repeatedly made clear in other sonnets and in the plays that Oxford believed Henry to be the legitimate heir to the throne. This also indicates that his marriage to Anne was a sham, a sacrifice to the Queen's political maneuvers. Anne Cecil de Vere was married in 1571, but it was not until 1575 when Oxford was in Italy, that she bore her first child, a daughter, Elizabeth. There is much confusion about Elizabeth de Vere's date of birth and there is considerable evidence that the child may not have been Oxford's at all. Lord Burghley wrote a memorandum on January 3, 1576 when he seemed to be justifying his "story" at a much later date:

> He [Oxford] confessed to my Lord Henry that he lay not
> with his wife, but at Hampton Court *(October 1574)*, and
> that then the child could not be his . . .[3]

There is reason to think that the "bed-trick" was used to trap Oxford at Hampton Court. This is the identical scenario that Helena uses to capture Bertram in *All's Well That Ends Well*, and Mariana to win Angelo in *Measure For Measure*. (The

Ogburns have noted that "Mariana of the moated grange" may be translated to "married Anne of the moated grange" at Theobalds, Burghley's magnificent estate.) Mariana, betrothed for five years to the elusive Angelo, arranges for Isabella to make an assignation with Angelo. However, it is Mariana who meets him, and in the dark Angelo unwittingly makes love to his own betrothed bride. Since Oxford recorded many of his own experiences in his plays and even incorporated this particular incident in two plays, it seems more than likely that this is a true account of what happened to him.

The story also appears in Thomas Wright's *A History and Topography of The County of Essex* written in 1836. He writes that Lord Oxford:

> ...forsook his lady's bed, (but) the father of Lady Anne by a stratagem contrived that her husband should unknowingly sleep with her, believing her to be another woman...[4]

Anne, in a letter to Lord Chamberlain Sussex, which by its circumlocutions and obsequiousness sounds as though it had been dictated by Lord Burghley, requests that rooms be reserved at Hampton Court for her in October, 1574. Note that Anne signs off, "From my father's house:"

> My good Lord, Because I think it is long since I saw Her Majesty, and would be glad to do my duty after Her Majesty's coming to Hampton Court, I heartily beseech your good Lordship to show me your favor in your order to the ushers for my lodging; that in consideration that there is but two chambers, it would please you to increase it with a third chamber next to it, which was reserved last

time for my Lord Arundel's men, and, as I was informed by my Lord Howard, he had it when he lay in the same lodging. I shall think myself bound to you for it, for the more commodious my lodging is the willinger I hope my husband will be to come thither, thereby the oftener to attend her Majesty. Thus trusting in your Lordship's favorable consideration I leave to trouble your Lordship any further, with my most hearty commendations to my good Lady, your wife. *From my father's house at Theobalds.*

Your Lordship's poor friend,
Anne Oxenford [5]

Considering all of the foregoing, it seems as though Anne Cecil de Vere, under the guidance of her wily father, did indeed set a trap to capture her elusive husband and, what is more, she succeeded.

It does seem to confirm, though, that Oxford had not consummated his supposed marriage to Anne up to this time. The earl, who attempted to pattern his life on Castiglione's *The Courtier,* would not have made a committment to the Queen and then lived with Anne as his wife. Anne, on the other hand, seems to have been naively unaware that she was being used as a pawn in a multinational game to establish a balance of power. Though the "bed trick" was used to catch Oxford in October of 1574, Anne was evidently not pregnant when Oxford left for the continent.

Oxford departed from England on January 5, 1575, arranging his affairs before he left. Since travel at that time involved a considerable element of risk, Oxford drew up papers leaving most of his estate, in the event of his death, to his cousins Horatio and Francis Vere. This is one more indication that he did not feel any obligation to Anne Cecil; on the contrary, he seemed to be making sure that the Cecil family were excluded from any possibility of inheriting the de Vere estate.

Lord Burghley was tenacious, however. He reasoned that if Anne Cecil de Vere were with child by Oxford before he left England, then that child would have a legitimate claim to the de Vere estates. If that child were a boy, he would also inherit the earldom. The incident at Hampton Court seems to have been initiated with this possibility in mind. However, according to Oxford's statement before his departure, Anne was not an expectant mother when he left for the Continent.

The confusion of dates surrounding the birth of Anne's daughter Elizabeth, and the correspondence relating to it, gives rise to a strong suspicion that the child could not have been Oxford's. It was not until the end of March that word was sent abroad to the supposed father that his wife was expecting. Anne herself made a telling comment that was quoted by one of the Queen's physicians, Dr. Masters, in his letter to Lord Burghley on March 7, 1575, describing details of his interview with Anne in the Queen's presence:

> Alas, alas, how should I rejoice seeing that he that should rejoice with me is not here: and to say truth (I) stand in *doubt whether he pass on me and it or not;* and bemoaning her case would lament that after so long sickness of body she should enter a new grief and sorrow of the mind. At this her majesty showed great compassion...And repeated my Lord of Oxford's answer to me, which he made openly in the presence of Her Majesty, viz., that *if she were with child it was not his*...Then she asking and being answered of me (who) was in the next chamber, she calleth my Lord of Le-

icester and telleth him all. And here I told her that though
your Lordship had concealed it awhile from her, yet you
left it to her discretion either to reveal it or keep it awhile
and lose. And here an end was made... (She said) that she
would be with you for concealing it so long from her. And
severally she showed herself unfeignedly to rejoice, and in
great offence with my Lord of Oxford, repeating the same
to my Lord of Leicester after he came to her. Thus much
rather to show my good will than otherwise desiring your
Lordship that there may be a note taken from the day of
the first quickening, for thereof somewhat may be known
noteworthy.[6]

In September of 1575 Oxford, then in Padua, Italy, received
the news from his father-in-law, Lord Burghley, that his wife
had been delivered of a daughter, Elizabeth, on July 2nd. It
was in response to this announcement that Oxford sent a Greek
Bible to his countess with a formal greeting and a Latin poem.
The poem filled with quibbles on *vera, veritas,* and the name
Vere, is given here in a translation by Captain B. M. Ward:

Words of *truth* are fitting to a Vere; lies are foreign to the
truth and only *true* things stand fast, all else is fluctuating
and comes to an end. Therefore since thou, a *Vere,* art wife
and mother of a *Vere* daughter, and seeing that thou mayst
with good hope look forward to being mother of an heir
of the *Veres,* may thy mind always glow with love of the *truth,*
and may thy *true* motto be *Ever* lover of the truth. And that
thou mayst the better attain to this, pray to the Author of
all *Truth,* that His word may teach thee: that His Spirit may
nourish thy inner life. So that, thus alleviating the longings
for thy dear absent husband, thou a *Vere,* mayst be called

the *true* glory of thy husband.[7]

This Latin poem shows early evidence of the earl's life-long use of word play on the Vere name. Sonnet 105 offers another example of this tendency to pun on his name and title.

It seems odd that Oxford showed no desire to return home to his wife on hearing of the birth of a child. Instead he wrote to his father-in-law, Lord Burghley, requesting permission to extend his stay in Italy. Not until the following spring did Oxford leave Italy and start home. He reached Paris on the return trip at the beginning of April.

There he was rejoined by one of his servants whom he had earlier sent back to England on a mission. Either from this retainer or from his cousins, the earls of Arundel and Howard, who were then on official business in Paris, Oxford learned the Court gossip that his wife was delivered of her child in September, not in July. In this case the child could not have been his. Burghley had done his best to convince Oxford that the child was his, but since the Queen, Leicester, and Dr. Masters all knew the story, it was probably well known by all at Court. Burghley's notes in his memorandum seem to be an attempt to reconstruct the time schedule.

Oxford had originally seemed quite pleased by the birth of a "child of my own" even though it might have confused the situation with Elizabeth and their son, whom she had taken from him. However, when the paternity of his daughter was questioned, his rage knew no bounds; he felt humiliated and dishonored by his wife's behavior. Worse still, the story seemed to be the common gossip of the Court. But worst of all was the possible implication of Burghley himself in the scandal.

As noted earlier, Burghley was little short of desperate for Anne to provide an heir to the Vere name and estate in case the earl met with a mishap on his journey. It is interesting, too, that Oxford's ship was attacked by pirates on his return from the Continent. Like Hamlet, he was lucky to escape with his life and, like Hamlet, he was sure that the incident was planned in order to dispose of him.

Oxford, on his return, refused to meet with either his wife or his father-in-law, and for several years he could not bear to see his wife or allow anyone to speak of her. Though they were eventually reunited and though she bore him three daughters and a son (the latter died soon after birth), he never quite trusted her or forgave her until after she died. Then he felt pangs of remorse for having treated her so badly, and yet these pangs were always combined with a lurking suspicion of her guilt.

Oxford's ambivalent attitude towards his wife is reflected in his portrayal of Ophelia in *Hamlet*. In Act II, scene 2, the seemingly mad Hamlet speaks to Polonius (Burghley), of his daughter, Ophelia (Anne):[8]

> Hamlet: For if the sun breed maggots in a dead dog, being a god kissing carrion - Have you a daughter?
> Polonius: I have my lord.
> Hamlet: Let her not walk i' th' sun. Conception is a blessing, but not as your daughter may conceive. Friend, look to't.

A passage in *King Lear* indicates that Oxford had equally strong feelings about Lord Burghley's involvement in this ugly situation. In Act III, scene 4, lines 51-55, Lear explodes in a violent execration:

> Lear: ...Tremble thou wretch,
> That hast within thee undivulged crimes
> Unwhipp'd of justice. Hide thee, thou bloody hand;
> Thou per'jur'd and thou simular of virtue
> That art incestuous.

Oxford deals with the incest theme again as the main plot of *Pericles*. It does seem as though it were important for him to deal with themes in his plays that were tormenting him in real life as a means of exorcising his troubles. Like other sensitive geniuses, he transformed his anguish into artistic creations. As Heinrich Heine, the great German poet, modestly observed, "Out of my great sorrows, come my little poems." Oxford's suffering, which was almost continuous from this point on, was transformed by his genius into the deathless verse and drama of the "Shake-speare" canon.

These years of the mid-1570s saw Oxford's life change from one that had been filled with glamor, opulence, and great prospects in his early years to a life-long struggle with adversity and heartache that would cease only with his death in 1604.

4 ❦ MAD IN PURSUIT

IN SPITE OF the terrible stress and disappointments of the 1570s, Oxford still hoped for a brighter future, and he continued to enjoy his privileged status with Elizabeth. Therefore, though aware of the awkwardness of his shadowy role, he felt great pride in the expectation that one day his son would be king. Perhaps he saw himself as Banquo, fated never to wear the crown but destined to sire a long line of kings.

Nevertheless, while Oxford continued to be a favorite of the Queen, Christopher Hatton held Elizabeth's interest, too. Hatton fawned and flattered unceasingly, while Elizabeth, in turn, was affectionate with him and called him her "sheep." Others referred to him less kindly as a "frippery gentleman" and the "dancing chancellor."[1]

Distressed by the Queen's obvious attachment to Oxford, Hatton appealed to his friend Edward Dyer for advice in coping with his rival.

Dyer's written reply is not only remarkably outspoken about his Sovereign but devious in its recommendations to the Lord Chancellor:

> First of all you must consider with whom you have to deal and
> what we be towards her; *who though she do descend very much in*

her sex as a woman, yet we *may not forget her place,* and the nature of it *as our Sovereign.*[2]

The conclusion of the letter warns Hatton to be circumspect about antagonizing Oxford, the Lord Chamberlain:

> ... hating my lord Ct(h)m in the Queen's understanding for affection's sake, and blaming him openly for seeking the Queen's favour ... Marry, thus much I advise you to remember, that you use no words of disgrace or reproach towards him to any; that he being the less provoked, may sleep, thinking all safe, while you do awake and attend to your advantages.[3]

In spite of this careful advice, Hatton seemed unable to restrain himself. In writing to thank the Queen for a gift he ends his letter with a vicious jab at Oxford:

> ...God witness I feign not. It is a gracious favor most dear and welcome unto me: *Reserve it to the Sheep* (Hatton), *he hath no tooth to bite,* where *the Boar's* (Oxford's) *tusk may both raze and tear.*[4]

Oxford's position close to the Queen allowed him to enjoy special privileges, and he evidently had the opportunity to read such private correspondence. Perhaps the Queen shared her letter with Oxford, and perhaps together they laughed at her ambitious admirer. Oxford had his chance to retaliate in *Twelfth Night*. An exchange of witticisms between Sir Andrew Aguecheek and Sir Toby Belch has no relation to the plot but seems to have been inserted for the amusement of the Queen and the Court, as well as the discomfiture of Hatton.

> Sir Andrew: ...and yet I will not compare it with an old man.
> Sir Toby: What is thy excellence in a Galliard Knight?
> Sir Andrew: Faith, I can cut a caper.
> Sir Toby: And I can cut the mutton to it.

He uses the Queens' pet name for Hatton but altered to 'Mutton,' which is an aged sheep, because he was ten years older than Oxford. The second line refers to Sir John Perrot's comment that "Hatton had danced his way into Elizabeth's heart on a Galliard." A caper is both a small legume that is an adjunct to a mutton sauce and a leaping vault in a Morris Dance; (like Macbeth, "his vaulting ambition o'er-leaps itself/And falls on th' other side"). One can imagine the seething fury of Mutton/Hatton on hearing this exchange and the hilarity of the rest of the Court.

However, Oxford was not overly concerned about a rival for Elizabeth's affection at this point. He was in fact, caught up in a passionate love affair with one of the Queen's young Maids-of-Honor, Anne Vavasour, who was a member of the innumerable Howard clan and therefore kin to Elizabeth. In 1578 Oxford wrote a poem for black-haired Anne, the first one addressed to the "Mysterious Dark Lady of the Sonnets."

Anne Vavasour's Echo

O Heavens! who was the first that bred in me this *fever? Vere.*
Who was the first that gave the wound whose fear I ware *forever? Vere.*
What tyrant, Cupid, to my harm usurps thy golden *quiver?*
Vere.
What wight first caught this heart and can from bondage it

deliver? Vere.
Yet who doth most adore this wight, oh hollow caves tell *true?*
You.
What makes him not regard good will with some regard of
truth? Youth.
What makes him show besides his birth, such pride and such
untruth? Youth.
May I his favor match with love, if he my love will try? Ay.
May I requite his birth with faith? Then faithful will I die? Ay.
    And I that knew this lady well,
    Said, Lord how great a miracle,
    To hear how *Echo told the truth,*
    As *true as Phoebus* Oracle.

Scholars have established that Elizabethan pronunciation was similar to a modern day Irish brogue. Therefore, 'fever' and 'Vere' would both rhyme with 'Fair' (as in the "fair Youth" of the sonnets).

Quick witted, tart-tongued, and vivacious, Anne Vavasour had captivated Oxford. In anguish, but fascinated by her, he could not leave her alone. Sonnet 129 expresses his torment:

    Mad in pursuit, and in possession so;
    Had, having, and in quest to have extreme;

From 1578 on Oxford's passion for Anne grew. He poured forth his emotions in a series of sonnets that have long been known as the "Dark Lady Sonnets." These may be divided into different categories that correspond with the progress of their love affair.[5] Sonnet 107 is a transition from Oxford's old love to his new, a comparison of Anne to Elizabeth.

In the old age black was not counted fair,
Or if it were, it bore not beauty's name;
But now is black beauty's successive heir;

"Beauty" is a nick-name for Elizabeth, and, therefore, "black" Anne is the successor to Elizabeth in Oxford's affections.

The tone of the earlier sonnets of the pleading category is that of the cajoling lover, while the later ones have the bitter, sardonic quality of a man who is angry with himself for loving someone unworthy of his love. However, being unable to resist her charms, he still pleads for favor. Sonnet 147 clearly expresses Oxford's ambivalence as his relationship with Anne progressed from flirtation to a serious involvement.

Past cure I am, now reason is past care,
And frantic-mad with evermore unrest;
My thoughts and my discourse as madmen's are,
At random from the truth vainly express'd
For I have sworn thee fair, and thought thee bright,
Who art as black as hell, as dark as night.

This is the cry of a desperate man who cannot seem to help himself. He has lost control and for a man of high ideals, who has tried to model himself on Castiglione's *The Courtier*, his is a terrible dilemma. But worse was yet to come. In March of 1581 Anne Vavasour gave birth to a son in the chambers of the Queen's Maids-of-Honour. Elizabeth, always a jealous guardian of her young attendants' chastity, was outraged. Like Julietta in *Measure For Measure*, Anne was disposed of to "Some more fitter place; and that with speed," for she was sent to the Tower when her child was less than a day old. The earl of Oxford, admitting his paternity, made a generous settlement of money and property on his son, who was later named Edward Vere. But Oxford's involvement in the affair stirred Elizabeth to an even greater fury, for her rage was now compounded by jealousy in his defection. Oxford was marched off to the Tower and, like Claudio in *Measure For Measure*, he was escorted under guard through the public streets:

> Claudio: Fellow, why dost thou show me thus to the world?
> Bear me to prison where I am committed.

It must have been a cruel humiliation for Oxford, the proud Lord Great Chamberlain, to be treated like a common criminal. All the bitterness, remorse, and anguish of Oxford's disgrace are expressed in Sonnet 129, but at the same time there is a new awareness of the human condition:

> Mad in pursuit, and in possession so,
> Had, having, and in quest to have, extreme,
> A bliss in proof, and prov'd, a very woe,
> Before, a joy propos'd; behind a dream.
> All this the world well knows, yet none knows well
> To shun the heaven that leads men to this hell.

Oxford spent the next three months in the Tower. The sonnet above was undoubtedly penned while he was incarcerated and seething with anger at himself. However, he was even more furious with Elizabeth, who was guilty of not one, but a number of infidelities. *Measure for Measure*, an enigmatic play labelled a "dark comedy" by puzzled scholars, is, in reality, Oxford's angry thrust at Elizabeth's hypocrisy.

On June 8, 1581 Oxford was released from the Tower and allowed to return home, but he was exiled from the Court for an indeterminate period. The Queen, approaching fifty and past her prime, had suffered a severe blow not only to her pride but to her plans for the succession. She had felt that Oxford was so high-minded, so honorable, that she could depend on his devotion to her. There were special bonds between them; Oxford's vows, their royal son and his idealism set him apart from the fawning Courtiers who sought favors from her. Though Elizabeth might wander in her affections, she had been sure that Oxford, who had sworn to be "Ever True," would remain so to the death.

In July of 1581, a month after his release from the Tower, Oxford wrote to his father-in-law, Lord Burghley, about his possible reinstatement at Court:

Robin Christmas (one of his two chief estate agents) did yesterday tell me how honorably you had dealt with Her Majesty as touching my liberty and that this day she had made promise to your Lordship that it shall be. Unless your Lordship shall make some motion to put Her Majesty in mind thereof, I fear in these other causes of the two Lords[6] she will forget me. For she is nothing of her own disposition, as I find, so ready to deliver as speedy to commit, and every little trifle gives her madder for long delay ...The world is so cunning *as of a shadow they can make a substance,[7] and a likelihood a truth* ...I must not forget to give your Lordship those thanks which are due to you for this your honourable dealing to her Majesty on my behalf, which I hope shall not be without effect. The which attending from the Court, I shall take my leave of your Lordship, and rest at your commandment at my house this morning.

Your Lordship's assured,
Edward Oxenford[8]

A letter to Lord Burghley from Sir Francis Walsingham on July 14, 1581 shows that Burghley had enlisted him to plead Oxford's case:

> I dealt very earnestly with the Queen touching the Earl of Oxford's liberty, putting her in mind of her promise made both to your Lordship and to the Lady his wife. The only stay growth through the impertinent suit which is made for the delivery of the Lord Howard and Master Charles Arundel, whom, before their delivery, Her Majesty thinketh meet they should be confronted by the Earl, who hath made humble request to be set at liberty before he be brought to charge them, as he was at the time he first gave information against them. Her Majesty, notwithstanding the reasonableness of the request, and the promises made to your Lordship ... cannot as yet be brought to yield ...[9]

Burghley also enlisted the aid of Christopher Hatton to speak for Oxford. Since there is no question that Burghley knew of the enmity between Oxford and Hatton, it is hard to understand Burghley's motive in approaching Oxford's rival to intercede for him with the Queen. Hatton not only hated Oxford but was close to Arundel and was, in fact, receiving letters from the latter signed "Your honor's fast and unfeigned friend."

Nevertheless, Burghley wrote Hatton on July 14th:

> ... yesterday, being advertised of your good and honourable dealing with Her Majesty in the case of *my daughter of Oxford*, I

could not suffer my thanks to grow above one day old; and therefore in these lines I do presently (immediately) thank you and do pray you in any proceeding therein not to have the Earl dealt with (con)stainably; but only by way of advice, as good for myself; for otherwise *he may suspect that I regard myself and my daughter more than he is regarded for his liberty.*[10]

It rather sounds as though Burghley were making a request that would suit himself and his daughter, not his son-in-law. Perhaps there was some stipulation in his request that involved Oxford being reunited with his wife. While it may have been simply a move of policy on Oxford's part, Burghley could well have insisted that this must happen before he would plead Oxford's case with the Queen. Whatever induced Oxford to approach Anne, it is clear that during the summer of 1581 he wrote to her and raised some hopes of a reconciliation. Although no letters of his overtures survive, Anne's response was preserved by her father. On December 7, 1581, Anne Cecil de Vere wrote abjectly to her husband:

My Lord, in what misery I may account myself to be, that neither can see any end thereof nor any hope to diminish it. And now of late having had some hope in my own conceit that your Lordship would have renewed some part of your favour that you began to show me this summer, when you made me assured of your good meaning, though you seemed fearful to show it by open address. Now after long silence of hearing anything from you, at the length I am informed—but how truly I know not and yet how uncomfortably I do not seek it— that your Lordship is entered into disliking of me without any cause in deed or thought. And therefore, my good Lord, I beseech you in the name of that God, which knoweth all my thoughts and love towards you, let me know the truth of your meaning towards me; upon what cause you are moved to continue me in this misery and what you would have me do in my power to recover your constant favour, so as your Lordship may not be let *still to detain me* in my calamity *without some probable cause,* whereof, I appeal to God, I am utterly innocent. From my father's house at Westminster.[11]

The phrases in italics seem to be legal terminology that would not roll off the tongue of a young woman in the sixteenth century. However, Lord Burghley, trained at the Inns of Court, would speak this way automatically, just as his son-in-law so often did. Legal language was so ingrained in them that such phrases were used without conscious thought.

Therefore, this letter sounds very much like Lord Burghley and, if not actually dictated by him, it was quite obviously written under his guidance. Oxford must have sent a reply immediately for Anne wrote another letter to her husband just six days after the first one. Again, Oxford's letter has been destroyed but Anne's has been carefully preserved:

My very good Lord, I most heartily thank you for your letter, and am most sorry to perceive how you are unquieted with the uncertainty of the world, whereof I myself am not without some taste. But seeing you will me to assure myself of anything that I may as your wife challenge of you, I will the more patiently abide the adversity which otherwise I fear, and—if God will so permit it that it might be good for you—I would leave the greater part of your adverse fortune and make it my comfort to bear a part with you. *As for my father, I do assure you, whatever hath been reported of him, I know no man can wish better to*

you than he doth, and yet the practices in Court I fear do seek to make
contrary shows.

...Good my Lord, assure yourself it is you whom only I love
and fear, and so am desirous above all the world to please you,
wishing that I might hear oftener from you until better fortune will have us meet together.[12]

While the countess of Oxford was devoted to her elusive husband, he continued to avoid the Cecil overtures. The rebuttal, shown
in italics, must have been the response to some complaint in Oxford's
letter of Burghley's self-serving treatment of Oxford. Thus,
Oxford's letter was expunged from the record. Had the letter shown
Burghley as Oxford's protector, it might have survived. Also Oxford may have been playing a poker game, implying that he would
live with Anne if Burghley could restore him to the Queen's favor,
but he was out-matched by Cecil, who must have had some sort of
leverage to force Oxford to accept Anne as his wife.

Oxford finally gave in; he must have felt for some reason that
he had no other choice. It was reported that "the Earl hath company with his wife since Christmas"[13] and Burghley had won the
match. Despite this, however, Oxford's suit to be allowed to return
to Court made no progress. Burghley had no intention of letting
Oxford return to Court and desert Anne again. Instead, the Court's
animosity and vengeance came to Oxford in the form of Anne
Vavasour's uncle, Thomas Knyvet.

Knyvet was a gentleman of the chamber, who was named
Keeper of Westminster Palace in January of 1582. About a month
later Knyvet challenged Oxford to a duel. Though the Queen had
several years earlier refused to allow Oxford to fight with Philip
Sidney on the grounds that an Earl was too much above a gentle-

man in rank, she now seemed to encourage her gentleman cousin Knyvet to avenge the wrong done to his niece and her cousin Anne Vavasour. Of course, it was not her concern for Anne but her wounded pride and her jealousy that motivated her. There was another far greater reason, too.

Elizabeth could not have him tried for treason without exposing her secret son and heir, Southampton, and, to further complicate the situation, Oxford was now living with Anne Cecil as his wife. Lord Burghley had done everything possible to maintain the fiction that Oxford had been the father of Elizabeth Vere. He had now succeeded in maneuvering Oxford into living with Anne, thus helping to give the illusion that their separation had been only temporary and that Elizabeth Vere was really Oxford's child. This new arrangement was perfect for Lord Burghley but compromised Oxford's situation with the Queen and left the Queen's plans for the succession in jeopardy. Therefore, some method of disposing of Oxford entirely was her only solution.

The timing of Knyvet's appointment as Keeper of Westminster just a month earlier suggests that this plum was his payment for the attack on Oxford. Surely if he waited a whole year before making his strike, it could not have been inspired by hot anger. It seems, rather, that there was a calculated purpose that drove him to attack Oxford. It must have been done by order of the Queen. Oxford had made too many mistakes, the affair with Anne Vavasour was hard to forgive, but living with Anne Cecil, to whom he had been pseudo-married, made the situation impossible. In order to claim the throne for Southampton, Oxford had to be removed immediately, before he had a family by Anne Cecil. Oxford's moving in with Anne at Christmastime, 1581, only served to bring the situation to a crisis. Elizabeth acted fairly quickly to have him eliminated in as subtle and logical a way as possible. Advanced in years and beyond child-bearing, Elizabeth was in a quandary. A statute had been passed in parliament in the early years of her reign that only "a child of her body might succeed her to the throne." Though Elizabeth could not send Oxford to the block as her father had done with her own mother, she must have felt a dynastic need to clear the way for her son. Thus we find on March 17, 1582 Nicholas Fant writing to Anthony Bacon that:

> In England of late, there hath been a fray between my Lord of Oxford and Master Thomas Knyvet of the Privy Chamber, who are both hurt, but my Lord of Oxford more dangerously. You know Master Knyvet is not meanly beloved in Court, and therefore *he is not likely to speed ill* whatsoever the quarrel be.[14]

Oxford, nearly killed in the duel, finally recovered after many months but was "by limping sway disabled" for the rest of his life.[15] Yet Elizabeth remained unyielding. With so much at stake it is not surprising that it took more than two years for Elizabeth to permit Oxford's return to Court.

On May 9, 1583 the earl and countess of Oxford had a son but the baby died a short time later. Perhaps because of the Queen's sympathy with Oxford's new sorrow or perhaps because there was a new favorite at Court, Walter Raleigh, to plead his cause, Elizabeth finally gave in. Raleigh's direct country ways quickly cut through the webs of intrigue and opened the way for Oxford's audience with the Queen.

> Her Majesty came yesterday to Greenwich from the Lord Treasurer's ... The day she came away, which was yesterday, the Earl of Oxford came into her presence and after some *bitter words and speeches,* in the end all sins are forgiven, and he

may repair to the Court at his pleasure. Master Raleigh was a great mean herein, whereat Pondus[16] is angry that he could not do so much.[17]

Perhaps Pondus / Burghley was angry not because "he could not do so much," but rather because he had accomplished too much. He knew well his daughter would be distressed to lose Oxford to Elizabeth again; he also had a need to cover his own past sins by keeping the pair together.

The Queen and her son Henry would always have first claim on Oxford. Oxford must have written several sonnets to Elizabeth some time before their reunion on June 1, 1583. Perhaps his poetic appeal had as much effect on the Queen as Raleigh's pleas, perhaps more. Sonnet 89 surely would have softened the most obdurate heart and perhaps it would have touched the Queen's conscience as well:

> Say that thou didst forsake me for some fault,
> And I will comment on that offense:
> Speak of my lameness, and I straight will halt,
> Against thy reasons making no defense.
> Thou canst not, love, disgrace me half so ill,
> To set a form upon desired change,
> As I'll myself disgrace: knowing thy will,
> I will acquaintance strangle and look strange;
> Be absent from thy walks; and in my tongue
> Thy sweet beloved name no more shall dwell,
> Lest I, too much profane, should do it wrong
> And haply of our old acquaintance tell.
>   For thee, against myself I'll vow debate,
>   For I must ne'er love him whom thou dost hate.

Oxford refers in this sonnet to the injury suffered in his duel with Knyvet. He draws on Elizabeth's sympathy by reminding her that she is responsible for having allowed the duel to take place. He will treat her like a stranger if that is her wish, yet he cannot resist reminding her that he could reveal much about their "old acquaintance" and all that he could tell of her own sins and hypocrisy. This sonnet shows a close relationship to *Measure For Measure*, the angry play that really does tell of her hyprocrisy. In Sonnet 26 Oxford speaks in a more humble mode and addresses the Queen in formal terms as his feudal lord:

> Lord of my love, to whom in vassalage
> Thy merit hath my duty strongly knit,
> To thee I send this written embassage,
> To witness duty, not to show my wit:
> Duty so great, which wit so poor as mine
> May make seem bare, in wanting words to show it,
> But that I hope some good conceit of thine
> In thy soul's thought (all naked) will bestow it;
> Till whatsoever star that guides my moving
> Points on me graciously with fair aspect
> And puts apparel on my tattered loving
> To show me worthy of thy sweet respect.
>   Then may I dare to boast how I do love thee
>   Till then not show my head where thou mayst prove me.

The Queen is not only his feudal overlord but she also rules his love. Oxford's duty to Elizabeth is two-fold: not only has she earned his fealty by love and parenthood, but he owes her his duty as her subject. Therefore, he is doubly bound to her; his bonds are stronger than any of her fawning courtier's. This sonnet is an "embassage," or formal ambassador, to affirm his duty to his sovereign, with no clever word-play, but bare truth. (He cannot resist word-play on witness, wit, and conceit, as a "witty conceit" or clever *conception*.)

Oxford depends on Elizabeth to provide the understanding in the depths of her soul, where her true thoughts are untainted by all of the lies fed her by the sycophants who surround her at Court. The "star that guides" him is not just astrological. It also refers to the star on the Oxford shield, the honored escutcheon of his noble ancestors, which should be his guide in upholding the honor of his ancestors as well as a shield to protect him.

Having used a metaphor of bareness, he speaks of putting on new apparel to cover his tattered loving. Until then he dare not show himself to her or tell her how much he loves her. Oxford humbly offers Elizabeth an image of a ragged beggar pleading for a scrap of pity and forgiveness.

While Oxford was writing "embassies" to Elizabeth, he was also writing sonnets addressed to the royal heir, Henry, at this time. As his life became more complicated and difficult, Oxford depended increasingly on this Tudor-Vere son as his main source of comfort. Sonnet 37 expresses the utter devotion to his Fair Youth:

> As a decrepit father takes delight,
> To see his active child do deeds of youth,
> So I, made lame by fortunes dearest spite,
> Take all my comfort of thy worth and truth,
> For whether beauty, birth, or wealth, or wit
> Or any of these all, or all, or more,
> Entitled in their parts do crownéd sit,
> I make my love engrafted to this store.

So then I am not lame, poor, nor despis'd,
Whilst that this shadow doth such substance give,
That I in thy abundance am suffic'd,
And by a part of all thy glory live.
    Look what is best, that best I wish in thee.
    This wish I have, then ten times happy me!

Though the allusion to lameness has often been passed off as figurative speech, it is in reality a bitter outcry against the dearest (expensive, in the sense that it cost him so much suffering) spite of Fortune. When one understands that Elizabeth was often referred to as "Fortune," the passage takes on new meaning. He blames Elizabeth's vicious spite for his being so cruelly maimed for life. "Worth" alludes to his son's standing as heir to the throne. "Truth" is his identity as a Vere, "beauty" represents Henry's relationship to Elizabeth, and his "birth" is Royal. Line seven confirms his royalty with further hints about his Entitlement and his Crown. The "shadow" of Henry's future glory gives such substance of hope to Oxford that he can abide his lameness and suffering. This echoes an almost identical phrase in his letter to Burghley (page 57); Oxford can bear his own trials by living vicariously in the future glory of his son as King.

In the 1570s, Oxford learned much about the world, particularly during his travels abroad on the Continent, but in the early 1580s he learned more about himself and the human condition.

His life and his outlook on life were changed forever. His sufferings, both physical and mental, had matured him. His great masterpieces, the history plays and tragedies, and the sonnets, henceforth reflected his new understanding.

Though much heartache lay ahead for Oxford, there were honors bestowed on him and considerable recognition of his accomplishments. Also, Oxford would play a key role in defending England from the long expected attack by Spain.

5 ❊ OUTWARD HONORING

WITH OXFORD'S RETURN TO COURT and the Queen's good graces, his life became a little easier. Surprisingly, though reluctant to accept Anne Cecil as his wife, he did not desert her again as Burghley had feared, and outwardly he seemed to be on good terms with his father-in-law. On April 6, 1584, Bridget was born and on May 26, 1587, Susan was born. At some time between the birth of Bridget and Susan another daughter, Frances, was born, but we have only the record of her death on September 12, 1587. Therefore, between May 1583 and May 1587 the earl and countess of Oxford had four children, though the son died almost immediately and Frances lived only a year or so. This would indicate that had Anne Cecil de Vere really been a wife to Oxford in the early years of their marriage, they would have had several children in the four years between their marriage in 1571 and the time when Oxford left for his trip to the continent in 1575. That Oxford would remain with Anne in this strange new situation is puzzling. His commitment to the Queen was somehow cancelled, but it is possible that Lord Burghley had some sort of holding power over Oxford, as he and his son Robert after him seemed to have over the Queen.

Whatever control Burghley used to maintain Oxford in this

odd dual condition, his personal life did seem calmer. However, Queen Elizabeth's situation was growing increasingly precarious. By 1585 it had become quite clear that as long as Mary Queen of Scots was held prisoner there would be an endless succession of plots to rescue her and put her on the English throne. However, it was the Babbington plot in 1586, which involved the proposed assassination of Elizabeth and most of the important members of her Court, that stirred the government to action. The Privy Council met to address the problem. Catholic members of the Council advocated more stringency in Mary's imprisonment; Leicester suggested disposing of her with poison. But Burghley, Walsingham, and others decided that a regular judicial inquiry was the proper procedure. Therefore, a commission was impaneled, on which Oxford served, to examine Mary at Fotheringay in Northamptonshire. However, the members were recalled to London after only two days of hearings. Elizabeth was vacillating for she was always aware of her own danger and afraid to set the precedent of sending an anointed sovereign to the block.

Nevertheless, when Parliament convened in October, the first order of business was the disposition of the dangerous captive queen. They voted by act of Parliament that Mary should be executed, but Elizabeth still refused to sign the order for the beheading. She tried in vain to pass the responsibility on to the Privy Council and scolded them for being cowardly when they refused to help her. Finally the Queen:

> . . . after having procrastinated endlessly, sent a message to (Wm.) Davison, Walsingham's deputy (Walsingham being conveniently ill), requiring him to bring the death-warrant immediately, and then signed it along with other state papers, in a pleasant, almost casual fashion pretending she had forgotten

it was there. But a few moments later, as Davison was leaving, she called him back, ordering him to take it forthwith to Cecil (for the affixing of the Great Seal). "Do it secretly," she commanded, "for it may prove dangerous to me were it known before the execution actually takes place."...pacing up and down, (she) began to question if there were not some other way. In the end, Davison...took the death warrant to Burghley, who affixed the Great Seal. After this, there was much maneuvering and dodging of responsibility...The upshot was that the Council left Burghley to bear the brunt; and he, characteristically, shelved it onto Davison.[1]

Later the Queen blamed Davison for having slipped the warrant in with other papers and having obtained her signature by subterfuge. "The Queen fined him so heavily that he was ruined and banished him from Court, leaving him a broken man."[2]

After Queen Mary was executed in February, 1587, Elizabeth reacted with violent hysterics compounded of both anger and fear. She reasoned that if one queen could be dispatched so readily, another queen could easily follow. Elizabeth was fearful that if Spain and France joined together to avenge the death of Mary, Queen of Scots, nothing could save her or England from the invaders. In the eyes of many Catholics both in England and abroad, Mary, once Queen of Scotland and France and the Catholic granddaughter of Henry VIII's sister, had more claim to the English throne than Elizabeth. Philip of Spain also claimed, as Mary Tudor's widower, that he was still King of England. Therefore, Elizabeth had every reason to expect an attack from either country or both.

For the next year and a half Elizabeth's little island realm prepared for the expected onslaught of the great powers of Europe, Spain and France, both of which were strongly backed by the Catholic Church. Elizabeth's perilous situation was further aggravated by the many Catholic members of the nobility and the large portion of her subjects that remained faithful to "the old religion." It was critically important that these citizens be made to feel more English than Catholic in their loyalties while the country prepared to defend itself from the dreaded attack.

Since the vast majority of Elizabeth's subjects were illiterate, the most effective way to instill a sense of patriotism in all the people of England was to show them a dramatic panorama of their past history. Oxford had already written a few history plays, such as *The Victories of Henry V* and *Thomas of Woodstock*, and presented them at Court. It is quite likely that the queen recognized the power of Oxford's history plays as a means of stirring patriotic pride. Perhaps this was why on June 26, 1586, Queen Elizabeth signed a Privy Seal Warrant to grant £1000 per year to the earl of Oxford. Excerpts from this warrant are as follows:

> To the Treasurer and Chamberlains of our exchequer, Greeting. We will and command you of Our treasure...to deliver and pay...unto Our right trusty and well beloved Cousin the Earl of Oxford...the sum of One Thousand Pounds good and lawful money of England. The same to be yearly delivered and paid unto Our said Cousin at four terms of the year in even portions: and so to be continued unto him during Our pleasure, or until such time as he shall be by Us otherwise provided for to be in some manner relieved;...Our further will and commandment is that neither the said Earl nor his assigns nor his or their executors nor any of them shall be way of account, impress, or any other way whatsoever be charged toward Us, our heirs or successors...Given under Our Privy Seal at Our Manor of Greenwich, the six and twentieth day of

June in the eight and twentieth year of Our reign.[3]

Elizabeth recognized Oxford's genius and felt his work must continue, not only for her own enjoyment but for the glory of her Court and her Country. Without her own discerning intellect and musical abilities there might never have been the great burgeoning of literature, music, and art in sixteenth century England or that wonder of all ages, Shake-speare.

Oxford, who had for some years been writing comedies and presenting them at Court, now in the 1580s turned to the production of history plays. Whether these were at the request of the Queen or were entirely Oxford's invention there is no way of knowing. The potential of these plays may have been evident to both of them as a means of affecting the hearts and minds of the citizens of England, both nobles and commoners alike. Whatever the origin, there now began that marvelous pageant of English history (from the Tudor point of view) known as the great Shakespeare history plays. Oxford, therefore, had a dual role in the preparation for the approaching war with Spain. A true Renaissance man, his dramatic and literary efforts would stir all England to fighting pitch. Later his "spear-shaking" abilities would also contribute to the actual fighting and the defeat of the Armada.

By 1588 the English were mobilized to defend the island, both on land and at sea. Disappointed not to be given a key role in the military preparations, Oxford nevertheless armed his small merchant vessel, the *Edward Bonaventure*, and stood ready to defend his queen and country. Leicester was commander-in-chief of the defending forces on land and Lord Howard of Effingham led the British naval forces at sea. Much as Oxford wished to serve in an important post, he was not only inexperienced but he was also "by limping sway disabled." Though offered a post as commander of the port at Harwich, he spurned the assignment and determined to join the fray in his own ship. John Lyly describes Oxford commanding his ship in a ballad about the Armada:

> De Vere whose fame and loyalty hath pearst
> The Tuscan clime, and through the Belgike lands
> By winged fame for valour is rehearst,
> Like warlike Mars upon the hatches stands.
> His tusked Boar 'gan to foam for inward ire,
> When Pallas filled his breast with warlike fire.[4]

When the battle was over and the Armada finally destroyed by a combination of the sheer chance of violent storms at sea and the clever naval tactics of the English fleet, wild rejoicing echoed throughout England. Though great celebrations followed, Oxford was so impoverished by supporting two acting companies and a handful of indigent writers, not to mention the suspect handling of his finances by Lord Burghley, that he was unable to honor his Queen's victory. This was a bitter humiliation for the proud Lord Great Chamberlain.

While Oxford was too poor to contribute to the celebrations, Christopher Hatton, on the contrary, was flourishing. Newly raised to the post of Lord Chancellor, Hatton entertained the Queen at a magnificent banquet on August 19, 1588 at Holborn. Hatton displayed himself in all his splendor, parading his hundred men-at-arms in red and yellow livery before the Queen and all the members of the Court. This was followed the next day by another elaborate dinner at Burghley's London home, Cecil House. Later that same day there was another review of troops at Leicester's grand mansion on the Thames. The day after, Essex had an even grander display for the Queen of mounted troops dressed in orange-tawny with white silk facings. It must have galled Oxford to think that he could provide nothing comparable to these displays to honor his sovereign.

A month later, in September, Elizabeth's triumph was turned to grief by the sudden death of the earl of Leicester, her long-time and very special favorite. However, after several weeks Queen Elizabeth decreed a solemn thanksgiving at St. Paul's on November 24 to celebrate the defeat of the Spanish Armada. Oxford's record of the event is found in Sonnet 125, when he held the position of honor in the Queen's triumphal procession from Somerset House to St. Paul's Church for the ceremony of Thanksgiving. Later, as the procession wound its way through the church, the earls of Oxford and Shrewsbury held a golden canopy over the Queen. B.M. Ward[5] tells of Oxford's part in the Queen's procession:

> An account of this great occasion has fortunately been preserved in the form of an anonymous ballad, which is of interest not only because of its vivid description of the event, but also because it tells us of the part taken by Lord Oxford.[6]
> An abbreviated version is quoted here:

> The Lord Marquess of Winchester bare-headed there was seen,
> Who bare the sword in comely sort before our noble Queen;
> *The noble Earl of Oxford then High Chamberlain of England*
> *Rode right before Her Majesty his bonnet in his hand.*
> *And after by two noblemen along the Church was led,*
> *With a golden canopy carried o'er her head.*
> The clergy with procession brought her Grace into the choir;
> Whereas her Majesty was set the service for to hear.

Stowe's Annals of 1615 records that Queen Elizabeth was:

> . . . under a rich canopy, brought through the long West aisle to her travers in the quire (choir), the clergy singing the Litany.[7]

Ward gives this account and provides a diagram of the Royal procession:[8]

> The Earl Marshall at this time was George Talbot, Earl of Shrewsbury. When we consider the places occupied by Oxford and Shrewsbury in the procession, there can be little doubt that they must have been the "two noblemen" who carried the Golden Canopy over her Majesty's head as she walked up the nave of St. Paul's and took her into the Choir. Moreover as Earl Marshall and Lord Great Chamberlain they ranked as the two senior Earls in the realm; and the only holder of a title higher than that of Earl at this time was the Marquess of Winchester, who carried the Sword of State.

Garter King at arms	The Mayor of London	A Gentleman usher of the Privy Chamber
Lord Great Chamberlain of England	*Sword Borne by the Lord Marquess*	*Earl Marshall of England*

The Queen's Majesty in her Chariot

Oxford was the Lord Great Chamberlain and Shrewsbury was Earl Marshall. In Sonnet 125 Oxford tells of carrying the Queen's canopy in the Royal procession and adds in line three that he has provided an heir that will carry the Vere/Tudor line on forever:

> Were't aught to me I bore the canopy,
> With my extern the outward honoring,
> Or laid great bases for eternity...

Oxford as well as Elizabeth had suffered a loss at this time. The death of Anne Cecil de Vere from a fever on July 5, 1588, just before the battle of the Armada, precipitated a crisis in Oxford's life and in his relationship with Lord Burghley.

At the time of Oxford's marriage to Anne, Burghley had seen to it that Castle Hedingham was assigned to Anne as her marriage portion. As long as she lived Oxford maintained Hedingham as his chief residence. Although his lifestyle during this period had been much reduced from the splendor he had known in his youth at Hedingham, he had not been in dire need. However, on Anne's death Burghley demanded not only custody of the three de Vere daughters, Elizabeth, Bridget, and Susan, claiming that Oxford was unfit to raise them, but also the guardianship and control of Castle Hedingham.

It is said that Oxford, outraged by the loss of his ancestral home and princely estate to the avaricious Lord Burghley, destroyed the castle. Although it was at that time an ancient structure, an old Norman fortress built by Aubrey de Vere in the time of William the Conqueror, it had been the home of the de Vere's for over four hundred years. But from 1588 on it has been an empty shell, a ruin. Today the outbuildings are gone and only the great Norman keep stands on a raised area, towering over the little village of Hedingham.

When settlement of all his accounts was demanded by Burghley in 1591, Oxford was left destitute. The loss of his great estate, his little kingdom, his heritage of four centuries of eminence, quite destroyed him. Furthermore, the loss of his daughters to Lord Burghley left him suddenly with neither home nor family. This was a bitter blow for a proud nobleman and an even greater suffering for a man of his sensitivity. King Lear's anguish is surely an echo of Oxford's own in Act III, scene 4, line 21:

Lear: O, that way madness lies; let me shun that.

In the earlier version of this play the King was "Leir," but in this tragic revision of the play the King's name is changed to become an anagram of "earl." The king/earl Oxenford almost goes mad with grief and anger when Burghley makes the last awful move to take Oxford's children and his birthright, his ancestral castle and home, from him. Not only does Burghley have Oxford's children by Anne living with him at Cecil House, but Henry Wriothesley, too. This would drive a sensitive man to the brink of madness, but Oxford, as usual exorcises his demons in his writing: King Lear, Act III, scene 2, lines 49-59:

Lear: Let the great gods,
    That keep this dreadful pudder[9] o'er our heads
    Find out our enemies now. Tremble, thou wretch,
    That hast within thee undivulged crimes,
    Unwhipped of justice. Hide thee, thou bloody hand;
    Thou perjur'd and thou simular of virtue
    That art incestuous. Caitiff, to pieces shake
    That under covert and convenient seeming
    Hast practis'd on man's life. Close pent-up guilts,

> Rive your concealing continents, and cry
> Those dreadful summoners grace. I am a man
> More sin'd against than sinning.

The line in the quotation above, "Tremble—Justice," which is addressed to Kent in the play, is in reality aimed at Lord Burghley. The lines "Hide—Incestuous" are again an outburst against Burghley.

"Caitiff" is classified as a rare word in the *Oxford English Dictionary*, which cites usage only by Oxford's uncle, the earl of Surrey, in his translation of the *Aeneid,* and by Shakespeare in *Othello.* However, it is also found in *Horestes*, an early play performed in 1567 and believed written by Oxford. Professor Kittredge translates the word "caitiff" as "wretch," but the O.E.D. also gives another meaning, "villain." This latter word seems more apt as used in this passage. "Caitiff—life" again charges Burghley, the villain, with hypocrisy and with sly dealings that have ruined Oxford's life. The use of "seeming" is a strong echo of Hamlet's antipathy to the word: "Seems, madam? Nay, it is. I know not 'seems'." Oxford, the true-telling idealist, scorns those who would dissemble. "Close—grace": close in on the hidden sins, break open the concealed evil hidden within you, appeal to those dreadful summoners for mercy. A "summoner" is an officer who calls offenders to an ecclesiastical court but is used here to call the offender on "The Day of Judgment" to answer for all his sins. Although Burghley's temporal power would protect him during his lifetime, Oxford warns him to prepare for that final Day of Judgment. At the same time Oxford recognizes his own frailties but feels that the wrongs he has suffered at the hands of others far exceed his own sins.

Another side of the king/earl speaks with the voice of the "wise fool." In Act III, Scene 2, the Fool observes, with an obvious play on "Headingham," that "He that has a house to put's *head in has* a good head-piece."

While King Lear speaks for Oxford's sorrows, his sonnets addressed to his son, Henry Wriothesley, speak for his one last hope. Sonnet 124 expresses Oxford's utter devotion to Henry and at the same time shows that he now has a clear-eyed view of Elizabeth's ruthless treatment of him:

> If my dear love were but the child of state
> It might for Fortune's bastard be unfather'd,
> As subject to time's love or to time's hate,
> Weeds among weeds, or flowers with flowers gathered.
> No, it was builder far from accident;
> It suffers not in smiling pomp, nor falls
> Under the blow of thralled discontent
> Whereto th' inviting time our fashion calls.
> It fears not Policy, that heretic,
> which works on leases of short-numbered hours,
> But all alone stands hugely politic...

If Southampton had been openly hailed as the heir to the throne, "Fortune" (Elizabeth) might have charged Oxford with treason for adultery and had him executed just as Henry VIII did with Elizabeth's mother, Anne Boleyn. He seems to understand exactly why he was attacked by Thomas Knyvet and that it was by order of the Queen. Though Elizabeth was a "Tudor Rose," she became a "weed" when her mother was beheaded and she, Elizabeth, was declared illegitimate. Henry Wriothesley, however, was hallowed by his parents' troth plight. Elizabeth was committed to providing a legitimate heir to the throne. However, Henry has escaped the fluctuations of parental interest that Elizabeth knew because he was never publicly recognized as the Tudor heir. Therefore, Henry is immune to any royal policy of the moment, yet he is at the same time "hugely politic" as the heir to the throne.

6 ✎ BEAUTY'S ROSE

IN THE ENSUING DECADE Oxford wrote many of the sonnets and his longer narrative poems for Henry Wriothesley. The love for his royal son served henceforth as the greatest inspiration for his poetry. Sonnets 1 through 17 not only express this paternal devotion and pride, but also they contain a royal parent's stern reminder to his son that he has a dynastic duty to perform. As the only surviving Tudor heir to the throne, he must marry and beget another generation to carry on the royal line:

That thereby *Beauty's Rose* might never die.

Bear in mind that "Beauty," (capitalized in the first publication of the sonnets), refers to Queen Elizabeth while the "Rose" (also capitalized) represents both the royal Tudor line and Henry Wriothesley as well. According to Southampton's biographer in 1925, Charlotte Stopes, his name was pronounced "Rosely."

In 1590 when Southampton was ostensibly seventeen years old, but in reality only sixteen, Lord Burghley began promoting a marriage between Henry and Elizabeth Vere, then 14 years old. Southampton at first did not refuse but pleaded for time to consider the matter, and there it rested for quite a while.

Henry must have known his true parentage by now and would have believed Elizabeth Vere to be his half-sister. However, both Lord Burghley and Oxford knew that she was not his sister at all. Oxford would have realized at this point that a marriage to William Cecil's daughter/granddaughter would strengthen Southampton's position as heir to the throne. It would be a triumph for Lord Burghley to see Elizabeth Cecil Vere queen of England when her husband became king. Fully aware of Burghley's lust for money, power and status, Oxford must have regarded this marriage as a guarantee of Southampton's future inheritance of the Crown. Bearing this in mind, Oxford wrote Sonnets 1 through 17 at this time to urge Southampton to marry Elizabeth Vere.

In Sonnet 2 Oxford warns his son what it will be like "When forty winters shall besiege thy brow," which suggests that this was Oxford's own age when writing these sonnets. Since he was born in 1550, this coincides with the year 1590, which was the time when Lord Burghley first began arranging Southampton's marriage to Elizabeth Vere.

In this series of sonnets Oxford repeatedly points out that his royal son is not a private person but belongs to the world. As such he must make a politic, arranged marriage in which personal preference is not to be considered. The message is clear: Henry Wriothesley has an obligation to fulfill, a duty to the English people to produce an heir to the throne. Nowhere is this more clearly stated than in Sonnet 1:

> From fairest creatures we desire increase,
> That thereby Beauty's Rose might never die,
> [...]
> Thou art now the world's fresh ornament,

And only herald to the gaudy spring,
Within thine own bud buriest thy content,
And, tender chorl, mak'st waste in niggarding:
    Pity the world, or else this glutton be,
    To eat the world's due, by the grave and thee.

"Fair" is used constantly in the sonnets as a variant of the name Vere (which was pronounced Vair). Henry was also fair in the sense that he was an extraordinarily handsome young man. Oxford urges him to marry and produce an heir to guarantee the continuation of the Tudor dynasty, represented by the Rose. "World's fresh ornament" indicates that Henry belongs to the world, (i.e. England's world). He may not think of himself as a private person, he has an obligation to produce another royal heir to succeed him. "Gaudy" may be read several ways: a "gaud" is a jewel (the queen's jewel); also the O.E.D. cites a Latin hymn beginning *"Gaude flore virginali"* (Rejoice in the flower of the Virgin), and "the gauds" were the large beads of the Rosary that served to mark the fifteen mysteries, the first five of which are the joyful mysteries including the birth of a babe to the Virgin Queen of Heaven. "Spring" in Latin is Ver. Henry is the only herald, or heir of Ver (spring). Henry, being young, though representative of the Tudor Rose, is still only a bud that will burst into full bloom when he becomes king. The last lines offer an image of the glutton eating what belongs to the world and completes the theme of increasing, growing, ripening (and famine from lack of a crop), and selfish eating imagery that starts with the first line of the sonnet.

Another example is worth looking at to demonstrate the urgency of the message in this group of "Procreation Sonnets." In Sonnet 14, Oxford seems holding the last thread of his tattered hopes in the future glory of his royal son.

> Not from the stars do I my judgment pluck,
> And yet methinks I have astronomy;
> [...]
> But from thine eyes my knowledge I derive,
> And, constant stars, in them I read such art
> As Truth and Beauty shall together thrive
> If from thyself to store thou wouldst convert;
>> Or else of thee this I prognosticate,
>> Thy end is Truth's and Beauty's doom and date.

The first quatrain claims that he is versed in astronomy but is unable to make great predictions for the future. "Astronomy" and "Astrology" were virtually synonymous in the sixteenth century. From the stars in the sky he turns to the "constant stars" of Henry's eyes; there he reads that Truth and Beauty (Oxford and Elizabeth, respectively) will live on in his progeny if he changes his ways to preserving rather than wasting himself. Then comes the dire warning that if Henry does not produce an heir, it will be the end of the Tudor-Vere dynasty. A late, more tragic, view of this situation is found in *The Phoenix and the Turtle* when in 1601 Oxford knows at last that "Truth and Beauty buried be."

In 1591 Queen Elizabeth visited Southampton at Tichfield. Just prior to her stay at Tichfield the queen had been entertained by Lord Montague at Cowdray from August 15 to August 21. There she was feted with much ceremony and pageantry, all of which was recorded in some detail by John Nichols in *The Progresses and Public Processions Of Queen Elizabeth.*[1]

Though we have surviving a very full account of the Royal visit to Cowdray we know practically nothing of the day or two that she spent at Tichfield. Burghley was with her and addressed a letter from there on September 2nd.

At this time Southampton was seventeen years old. We can only speculate why Elizabeth chose to make a private visit to her son. Since Lord Burghley was present, too, the purpose may well have been to urge Henry to marry Elizabeth Vere. The queen certainly knew that the girl was not Oxford's daughter, and she was fully aware of Cecil's ambitions. She, like Oxford, must have seen this union as a guarantee that the Cecils would promote Henry as her heir if it meant that a Cecil would be Henry's queen-consort.

While Burghley put pressure on Southampton to marry Elizabeth Vere, he also, in 1590, destroyed Oxford financially. As Lord Treasurer, he demanded of Oxford a final settlement of the earl's business with the Court of Wards. This was never pursued as long as Anne Cecil Vere was alive, but now that her protection was gone, William Cecil proceeded to glean everything he could from the forty-year-old premier earl of England. The financial demands Burghley made at this time are rather suspect. He not only claimed Castle Hedingham, as noted previously, but now presented Oxford with a staggering account of his debt to the Court of Wards:

Forfeitures, in the Court of Wards, £11,000
Forfeitures of Covenants upon the livery, £4,000
Upon his Wardship, £3,000
Other Obligation, £4,000 [2]

These claims by their very non-specificity and by their tardiness seem utterly specious. Since Lord Burghley had been managing Oxford's affairs all these years, it seems as though this situation should not and could not have really existed. Obviously Oxford would have no way of knowing about his accounts because his guardian/father-in-law had handled everything from 1562 until this terrible reckoning in 1590. It does seem as though Burghley licked the platter clean knowing that Oxford could say nothing.

Destroyed financially by these demands and devastated by the loss of Hedingham, Oxford was rescued by a wealthy young woman, Elizabeth Trentham, who was a maid-of-honor to the queen. She and Oxford were married in September of 1591. At 41, Oxford was an old man by sixteenth century standards, "beated and chopp'd with tann'd antiquity," and writes ruefully of the disparity in their ages in Sonnet 138:

> When my love swears that she is made of truth
> I do believe her, though I know she lies,
> [...]
> And wherefore say not I that I am old?
> O, love's best habits is in seeming trust,
> And age in love loves not to have years told.
>   Therefore I lie with her and she with me,
>   And in our faults by lies we flattered be.

"Truth" as always refers to Vere. Elizabeth Trentham has been made a Vere by her marriage.

Oxford knew all too well how false the world could be. Those whom he should have trusted most, the queen, his late wife Anne, and Lord Burghley, had all proved false to him. However, this last relationship with Elizabeth Trentham provided him with a security and calm he had not known since he was a child, and it also allowed Oxford to escape from Lord Burghley's grasping fingers. Eventually the new countess of Oxford, who was a woman of considerable fortune, repurchased Hedingham from the Cecils. Not long after they were married she also bought King's Place, a comfortable mansion in Hackney well removed from Court but within easy reach of the theater district. Thenceforth, Oxford was free to devote his time to writing and to working in the theater.

While Oxford's life had suddenly become serene, Southampton was trying to fend off Burghley's marriage demands. At the same time, however, Henry was heartened by finally receiving attention from his mother, the queen.

7 ᘓᘓ FAIR LEAVES SPREAD

AFTER QUEEN ELIZABETH and Lord Burghley visited Southampton at Tichfield in 1592, Southampton subsequently attended Court quite regularly and accompanied Elizabeth on public occasions. In 1592 Southampton joined the queen on a trip to Oxford University. The university later published a Latin poem by John Sanford commemorating the Royal visit. The poem ended with a tribute to the young earl of Southampton:

> . . . a lord of lofty line whom rich Southampton claims in his own right as a great hero. There was present no one more comely, no man more outstanding in learning, although his mouth scarcely yet blooms with tender down.[1]

This seems excessive praise for a youth of seventeen, though not uncommon when addressing a man of rank. It is more understandable, however, if his true heritage were known, and there did seem to be many who were in on the secret in the 1590s. Ben Jonson knew it well, as evidenced by his snide burlesque of the "Royal Family" in *Bartholomew Fair*, a play written in 1596 but never performed until 1614. The action of the play centers on the tent of the Pig-woman Ursa, where she specializes in roast pig. Her assistant is a young boy known as Moon-calf. Ursa, Latin for "bear," is the insignia of the goddess Diana and, since Queen Elizabeth was constantly referred to as Diana, goddess of the moon, it takes just one small step more to recognize 'Ursa' as a crude depiction of the Queen. "Moon-calf" is equally telling; his name simply combines designations for Elizabeth and for Oxford, the moon for Elizabeth, and the calf, or young Ox, for Oxford.

In Shakespeare's *2 Henry IV*, Act II, scene 4, line 205, Doll Tearsheet, speaking to Falstaff, addresses him as "Thou whoreson little tidy Bartholomew boar-pig." Ben Jonson in *Bartholomew Fair*, Act I, scene 6, line 50, also speaks of the Bartholomew pig:

> . . . it may be eaten . . . But in the Fair, and as a Bartholomew-pig, it cannot be eaten, for the very calling it a Bartholomew-pig, and to eat it so, is a spice of idolatry, and you make the Fair no better than one of the high places. This I take it, is the state of the question. A high place.

Jonson's Bartholomew Boar-pig cannot be eaten because it represents Vere (Fair). His allusion to "idolatry" echoes the first line of Sonnet 105: "Let not my love be called idolatry." Finally Jonson tells us that all of this exchange refers to affairs of State in high places. Though Jonson's caricature is colored by envy and resentment of those more fortunate than he, there are others who speak with sincere praise of Southampton and his family. In 1603, *A Welch Bayte To Spare Provender* was published by Thomas Powell with a dedication to Southampton, which was highly complimentary and remarkably outspoken:

A Prelude upon the name of
Henry Wriothesley Earl of
Southampton

Ever

Whoso beholds this leafe, therein shall reade

A faithful subjects name, he shall indeede

The grey-eyde morne in noontide clowdes may steep

But traytor and his name shall never meete.

Never

The placement of "Ever" and "Never" makes a daringly pointed statement about Southampton's relationship to "Edward de Vere, seventeenth earl of Oxford. Also, "The grey-eyde morn...steep" seems to refer directly to Sonnet 33 and the line: "The Region (Regina) cloud hath masked him from me now."

Thomas Nashe was equally bold in his address to Southampton in his prologue to *Choice of Valentines*:

> Pardon sweete flower of matchless poetrie
>
> And fairest bud that red rose ever bore.

The meaning is plain. Nashe identifies Southampton as the flower of "Shake-speare's" matchless poetry, the little Western Flower of *Venus and Adonis*, and the Rose Bud of the Sonnets. Like Oxford, Nashe uses "Faire" for "Vere," "ever" for E. Vere" and the "rose" to represent Elizabeth. Nashe continues in the same vein:

> Ne blame my verse of loose unchastity
>
> For painting forth the things that hidden are

This seems to echo the plaint of *The Phoenix and The Turtle* in a most outspoken way. The Ogburns note that, "By the middle or late 1590s many people seem to have known the secret."[2] If Queen Elizabeth needed encouragement to name her son, Henry, as her successor, her subjects were providing it. Edward de Vere and his son, Henry Wriothesley, were beloved by many and those who knew their story seemed anxious to claim them as the Royal Family. However, the Cecils, father William and son Robert, greedy for wealth and power, ruthlessly maneuvered for control of Elizabeth and the succession. They managed to expunge the truth from the official records and to dispose of people who stood in their way.

While other poets were honoring Southampton, Oxford, too, was pouring forth love and praise for his son Henry. The two long poems, *Venus and Adonis* and *The Rape of Lucrece* were openly dedicated to Henry and many of the sonnets written during the 1590s were addressed to his beloved royal heir. Three sonnets that express the father-son relationship most explicitly are 39, 76, and 112. It is difficult to understand how anyone could misread the parental love expressed in these sonnets. The first quatrain of Sonnet 39 speaks for any proud father who sees the best of himself in his son:

> O, how thy worth with manners may I sing
> When thou art all the better part of me?
> What can mine own praise to mine own self bring?
> And what is't but mine own when I praise thee?

Only a parent can tell a child that he is "all the better part of" him. When the poet claims that if he offers praise to the addressee, that it is "praise to mine own self," he can only be speaking to his son. Another parental point of view is evident in Sonnet 112:

> Your love and pity doth th' impression fill
> Which vulgar scandal stamp'd upon my brow;
> For what care I who calls me good or ill,

So you o'er-green my bad, my good allow?

It is the eternal hope of each generation that the next generation will somehow succeed where they have not and will avoid the
pitfalls that have harmed their parents.

Sonnet 76 contains not only messages to his son but also mul-
tiple clues to identify both of the parents and their son:

> Why is my verse so barren of new pride?
> So far from variation or quick change?
> Why, with the time, do I not glance aside
> To new-found methods and to compounds strange
> Why write I still all one, ever the same,
> And keep invention in a noted weed.
> That every word doth almost tell my name,
> Showing their birth and where they did proceed?
> O, know sweet love, I always write of you,
> And you and love are still my argument:
> So all my best is dressing old words new,
> Spending again what is already spent;
>   For as the sun is daily new and old,
>   So is my love still telling what is told.

"Verse" in line one includes the name Vere, and "Variation" in
line two again repeats the Vere name with the "i" neatly adding the
"E" sound for Edward's initial. In line five, "All one" is a partial
representation of Southampton's motto, *"Ung par tout, tout par ung"*
(One for all, all for one), while "Ever the same" is Queen Elizabeth's
motto, "Semper Eadem" (Always the same), but with the synonymous "Ever" replacing "always" to allow for the inclusion of Oxford's
name. "The noted weed" is the wild or hidden royal Son, who is

repeatedly represented by the wild, or canker rose, or Eglantine. In line seven "every word" is almost an anagram for Edward Vere, as he tells us succinctly in the second half of the line, "almost tells my name." Indeed, every word of this sonnet clearly identifies the writer and his heritage as the noble Lord Great Chamberlain of England and father of Queen Elizabeth's royal heir.

"Sweet love" (his royal son), is identified at the end of line nine as "You" or "HUU" or "H.W." the "YOU/HUU" is also repeated in the next line. In line thirteen "Sun," often spelled the same as "son" originally, allows for a double reading of the word; Southampton was not only his son but was also, like the sun, the center of his universe. The first half of the 1590s found Southampton at the center of Court activities. He was widely recognized as the queen's prime favorite and it seemed only a matter of time before Elizabeth would present him to the world as her heir. Though Southampton remained in high favor with the queen for about five years, his behavior at Court was not the best. His petty squabbles and lack of consideration for others grew worse with time. He gambled constantly and lost large amounts of money. It must have been disheartening for the aging queen to realize that her son and heir seemed quite unfit to mount the throne and govern England. Even his doting father felt obliged to lecture him in Sonnets 95 and 96 where he sternly warns Southampton of his destructive behavior:

Sonnet 95

How sweet and lovely dost thou make the shame
Which, like a canker in the fragrant rose,
Doth spot the Beauty of thy budding name!
O, in what sweets dost thou thy sins enclose!

Sonnet 96

Some say thy fault is youth, some wantonness;
Some say thy grace is youth and gentle sport.
[...]
As on the finger of a throné d queen
The basest jewel will be well esteem'd...

However, Southampton ignored all warnings, and Elizabeth either tolerated his laxness or was unaware of his shortcomings. Undoubtedly he was on his best behavior in the queen's presence, and he continued in high favor until late October, 1595. Then she suddenly was quite abrupt with him:

My Lord of Southampton offering to help the Queen to her horse, was refused, he is gone from Court, and not yet returned.[3]

Southampton did return to Court in time for the November 17 anniversary celebration of Elizabeth's accession to the throne, and he was included among the Jousters in the "Queen's Day" Tournament. Akrigg reports that, "George Peele, writing a fine Spensesrian poem upon the occasion, gave high praise to 'young Wriothesley' whom he found 'gentle and debonair.'"[4]

Southampton's fall from grace may have been due to his paying too much attention to one of the queen's maids of honor, Elizabeth Vernon, a cousin of the earl of Essex. Elizabeth Vernon was one of numerous daughters of a recently deceased country squire, Sir John Vernon. Financially she was dependent on the earl of Essex whose mother, the former Lettice Knollys, was her aunt and through whom she received her appointment at Court. Since Lettice Knollys was a granddaughter of Mary Boleyn, (sister of Anne, the Queen's mother), this meant that both Essex and Elizabeth Vernon were Southampton's second cousins once removed. They were also great niece and great nephew to the queen. Relationships could get quite complicated among members of the nobility in sixteenth century England.

Rowland Whyte, writing Court gossip in late September of 1595, notes:

> My Lord of Southampton doth with to(o) much Familiarity court the faire Mistress Vernon . . . Her friends might well warn her that Southampton was indeed 'a prince out of thy star.'[5]

This warning, though possibly referring to a noble Lord, sounds more as though Elizabeth Vernon were being warned to stay away from the Royal Prince.

Though it was a fairly common occurrence, the Queen was always outraged when any of her Maids of Honor became involved with her Courtiers. In this instance there was more at stake. The queen knew all too well the dangers of Royalty following their hearts' desires. As Tudor heir, Southampton could not afford to be careless; he was expected to make a dynastic match, an arranged marriage.

While Southampton was carrying on this unsanctioned flirtation at home, he was also fretting because his cousin, the earl of Essex, was earning great honors in several military and naval campaigns. However, the queen would not allow Southampton to join these expeditions; presumably, it would be too great a risk for the only heir to the throne. In 1596 Essex achieved a brilliant success in an attack on the Spaniards at Cadiz. Returning laden with treasures, Essex was acclaimed as a hero. This was hard for

Southampton to endure. Just as his father had been frustrated by being kept at home in his youth, Southampton now longed to see action. In 1597 the queen's attitude seemed to change or perhaps she felt her son was safer in a military campaign than in the arms of Elizabeth Vernon. Whatever the reason, Southampton finally received permission to accompany his cousin Essex on an expedition to the Azores.

Intelligence reports received in England after Essex's successful attack on Cadiz revealed that the Spaniards were outfitting a fleet at Ferrol and Corunna in the Azores to avenge the damage done by the English, and they were also raising an army to invade England. Though more recent reports indicated that some terrible sickness had decimated the Spanish regiments and that storms had destroyed most of the fleet, the English forces continued their preparations. The plan was set to attack Ferrol, where the Spanish fleet was being refurbished.

The English campaign did not fare well from the start. As they set out, storms at sea caused much damage, which meant returning to England for repairs to the ships. When they set out a second time, they again encountered heavy storms and then a becalmed period. All in all it was a difficult excursion.

On arriving at Flores, the most westerly island in the Azores, Essex was advised by his naval officers, the chief of which was Lord Howard of Effingham, to spread his ships in a broad screen north and south. Being more of a soldier than a naval officer, Essex listened to his closest associates, who, like him, were soldiers all longing for a land battle. Too many of them had suffered from sea sickness in the storms at sea and they were anxious to fight with their feet on firm ground.

While Essex and his conflicting advisers were vacillating and trying to come to some agreement, the Spanish fleet slipped out of port and escaped. It was obvious to the English by now that the Spaniards were not to be taken by surprise. Therefore, they abandoned their plan to seize the capital of the island and instead attacked a smaller town down the coast, Villa Franca, where they "took tolerable booty."[6] Then, with autumn approaching and provisions running low, there was nothing for the English to do but head for home. Essex returned to England with little to show for his efforts, his reputation as a successful campaigner in shreds. Essex seemed to be like "the painful warrior" in Sonnet 25:

> Great princes' favourites their fair leaves spread
> But as the marigold at the sun's eye;
> And in themselves their pride lies buried,
> For at a frown they in their glory die.
> The painful warrior famousé d for fight,
> After a thousand victories once foil'd,
> Is from the book of honour rasé d quite.

While Southampton and Essex were campaigning in the Azores, Elizabeth had summoned one of her infrequent parliaments. On his return Southampton made his initial appearance in the House of Lords. Akrigg reports that:

> Somebody, perhaps Lord Burghley, took pains to draw Southampton into the business of the House, and he was appointed to no less than six committees . . . If Burghley had hoped that these appointments would make a diligent Parliament man out of Southampton he was disappointed. Southampton became a chronic absentee. He was present for only one of he twelve sittings of the Lords after the Christmas

vacation.[7]

If Burghley was at all involved in trying "to draw Southampton into the business of the House," surely it was by order of the queen. She must have wondered what she could do to turn her wastrel son into a statesman.

However, Southampton had other matters to distract him at the moment. His finances were in critical condition, due in part to high living and reckless gambling, but also to a great degree to Lord Burghley's depredations.

Lord Burghley had handled Southampton's estate while he was a ward of the Crown, and as always in that situation, the ward became impoverished while Lord Burghley waxed wealthy. In addition, Lord Burghley exacted a large fine of £5000 from Southampton when he finally refused to marry Elizabeth Vere. In order to satisfy his debts Southampton was obliged to sell manors in North Stoneham, Portsea, Copnor, Corhampton and Bighton. In hopes that living abroad quietly for two years might help to stabilize his finances, Southampton requested permission to go to the continent. However, there was considerable delay in getting the queen's official license to travel. It was undoubtedly a difficult decision for the aging queen to give permission to her only heir to leave the country for two years. At sixty-five she was an old woman in terms of a sixteenth century life span. From her own experience, she knew how important it was for an ascendant sovereign to be immediately available. It was critically important for her successor to be nearby when she was ready to go.

Slow as she was to make decisions, the queen finally, on February 6, gave Southampton his license to travel abroad for two years. Perhaps the queen felt that this would educate and mature him in preparation for his future role as monarch. She may have hoped, too, that he would forget his passion for her maid of honor, Elizabeth Vernon. Whatever her reasoning, she reconciled to his going. With him would go ten servants, six horses and £200. This, along with a letter of credit for 1000 crowns, was his financing for two years of travel.

Rowland Whyte, that inveterate reporter of Court gossip, noted that, "His (Southampton's) faire mistress doth wash her fairest face with many teares."[8] Evidently Elizabeth Vernon had good reason to be distressed. Southampton never travelled further than France. On or about August 30, 1598 he returned secretly to London and married Elizabeth, who was then six months pregnant. On September 3, when Southampton was on his way back to Paris, Queen Elizabeth learned of the marriage. Outraged, she promptly sent a letter to Sir Thomas Edmondes, her ambassador in Paris, ordering him to find Southampton and to return him immediately.[9]

Lord Burghley had died on August 4 and his son Robert took over the office of Secretary. Robert Cecil wrote to Edmondes in his official capacity. His letter, sent by the same post as the queen's, carried a "warning that Southampton would only make matters worse if he did not return promptly."[10] Meanwhile, the Queen's wrath fell on the unfortunate bride:

> now understand that the Queen hath commanded that there
> shall be provided for the novissima countess the sweetest and
> best appointed lodging in the Fleet (prison).[11]

After some delay, claiming that he had no money, Southampton finally returned to England. By the beginning of November Southampton was back in London and lodged in the Fleet Prison. A week later the new countess had a daughter, who was named

Penelope after Penelope Rich, the earl of Essex's sister, and the new mother's first cousin.

Essex did what he could to have Southampton released from prison as quickly as possible, but it took him until the end of November to accomplish it. For Southampton the crisis was over at last, but a far larger one loomed ahead.

8 ❈ EDGE OF DOOM

In August of 1598 Queen Elizabeth and her Privy Council were faced with a major crisis in Ireland. The Irish, long resistant to English rule, had quietly organized a large, well disciplined army with which they attacked an important English fort near the Blackwater River and won a stunning victory. In response to this, the rest of Ireland burst into open revolt. Before winter closed in, the English had lost control of most of Ireland with the exception of a few cities and castles. Worst of all, King Philip of Spain had sent officers to determine which ports would be best for landing Spanish troops equipped with artillery to help the Irish. Elizabeth and her Privy Council rushed to prepare troops for an Irish campaign to recover the land that had been lost and to re-establish English rule in Ireland.

There was much speculation and discussion about who would be appointed Lord Lieutenant of Ireland with the responsibility of putting down the rebellion and restoring order. If he were successful, the man appointed to the job would receive great honor and acclaim. However, Ireland was notorious as a place where Englishmen lost their reputations or were left and forgotten.

The Privy Council met to decide on a course of action and to choose a commander of the armed forces for the Irish campaign. The earl of Essex spoke up repeatedly to veto the choice of several possible commanders. At last the Council offered the job to Essex. Refusing at first, he finally agreed to take charge himself. Since Essex's advancement at Court had been thwarted by Robert Cecil and his supporters, he felt that his only chance for recognition was to achieve success as a soldier.

Rumor had it that Essex, on being named commander of the Irish expedition, immediately assigned the post of General of the Horse to his friend (and also his cousin and his cousin-in-law), the earl of Southampton. Although it was probably true that he had already unofficially promised it to Southampton, it was made clear early in 1599, in a private interview at Richmond, that the queen was against her son's appointment. She gave firm orders that he was not to have any command in the army preparing for Ireland. Undoubtedly she did not want him involved in the actual fighting, for she had made the same stipulation before allowing Southampton to accompany Essex on the Azores campaign.

Sorely disappointed, Southampton was assured by Essex that once he had his commission he would be empowered to appoint his own officers anyway, and "then if she quarrel with me, her wrong is the greater and my standing on it will appear more just."[1] Essex was brashly overconfident of his influence on the queen. She might be a doting aunt, but she also could be quite harsh with Essex on occasion:

> Though at times she could be gracious and kindly to Essex,
> she was more often nagging and shrewish.[2]

Actually it is rather surprising that Elizabeth favored Essex at all, for she bore no love for his mother, Lettice Knollys Devereaux Dudley Blount. Lettice had antagonized the queen many years earlier by marrying the earl of Leicester, Elizabeth's beloved "Robin." Then the queen felt that Lettice, the new countess of Leicester, was competing with her in splendor of dress and equipage. She had even boxed Lettice's ears when she appeared at Court gowned in satins and adorned with jewels, rivaling Elizabeth's magnificence.

Essex, however, was a handsome young man who was not only the queen's great nephew, but also had the advantage of an introduction to the Court by his step-father, the same adored Robin. Under Leicester's aegis, Essex enjoyed easy access to the queen and, from the start, an unusual degree of informality.

Six months after the Privy Council had met in August, Essex left London on March 27, 1599, taking with him Southampton, Lord Grey, Robert Cecil's close friend (and probably his spy), Lords Audley and Cromwell, as well as several hundred gentlemen volunteers. "After a short stop-over in Wales, where Essex and his officers were royally feted, the group sailed for Ireland."[3]

Arriving in Ireland, Essex was invested as commander on April 15. Then, quite contrary to the Queen's order, he appointed Southampton General of the Horse. This was his first important mistake.

Before leaving England Essex had presented a simple plan to the Queen and the Privy Council. Since the Irish had rebelled under the leadership of the earl of Tyrone, Essex planned to crush him first by making a quick foray into Ulster with his

16,000 foot soldiers and 1,300 horsemen. Following that, he would subdue the insurgents in the rest of the country.[4] However, on his arrival in Dublin, Essex found the job more complex than he had anticipated. He needed supplies for the troops and transports to move them. Furthermore, forage for the horses would not be available until June. Meanwhile, the English garrisons in Leinster and Connaught were sending urgent messages begging for help. Essex's hastily assembled army of recruits was not ready for battle, and the council in Dublin agreed that it was impossible to head north with the army at that time. Essex felt that he should first rescue the fort at Leinster, which was being threatened by the rebels, and then travel to the border of Munster to consult with the English authorities there. Before putting this new plan in action, Essex sent a full report to the queen and the Privy Council and received complete approval from them for his change of plan.

Essex, Southampton, the other officers and their troops campaigned in the south and west with great success, defeating the enemy in several battles. Then a message arrived from Sir Thomas Norris in Munster with a desperate plea for help. Responding, Essex led his troops west heading for Cahir Castle, one of the strongest Irish-held fortresses in the country. After a siege of the castle and a fierce battle, the English took the castle and the surrounding area. Though the Privy Council back in England did not recognize the importance of this victory, it was the cause of a number of Irish leaders dropping out of the rebellion.

Essex and his troops then continued westward, winning skirmishes as they moved through the countryside, and on June 10th they were in Askeaton when the long-delayed supply boats arrived up the river. Essex was in good spirits and all seemed well with the campaign. Shortly after this a devastating letter arrived from Robert Cecil:

> Her Majesty having of late received certain knowledge that your Lordship hath constituted the Earl of Southampton General of the Horse in her Majesty's army under your charge, with which she is much displeased, hath given us commandment to signify her mind in that behalf, and to let your Lordship understand that she thinketh it strange, and taketh it offensively that you would appoint his Lordship to that place and office, considering that her Majesty did not only deny it, when she was here moved by your Lordship to that purpose, but gave you an express prohibition to the contrary, that he should not be appointed thereunto. This commandment being (as her Majesty saith) so precisely delivered unto you, and the same being now so manifestly to the world to be broken, hath moved Her majesty to great offense in that respect. And therefore Her Majesty's pleasure is that you do no longer continue him in that place and charge of General of the Horse, but to dispose of it to some other, as you should think good. Her Majesty esteeming it a very unseasonable time to confer upon him any so great place, having so lately given her cause of offense towards him. This being Her Majesty's direction and commandment unto us, we do deliver it by this our letter as from herself, wherein having discharged our duties, we are sorry for the occasion.
>
> The Court of Greenwich, 1599, June 10.[5]

Since the queen had known for some time of Southampton's appointment, Cecil may have added his influence to authorize the "commandment," or perhaps it was not from the queen at all but was Cecil's order. The Queen had originally made it clear that Southampton was to have only a minor role in the Irish campaign, but Cecil now had his own good reason for removing Southampton from his position.

In one of Southampton's earliest encounters with the Irish rebels in the south, Lord Grey had disobeyed Southampton's orders, wildly pursuing enemy troops. Since it had long been a favorite Irish trick to lure the English troops into their treacherous bogs, it could have been a costly disobedience. Southampton had rescued Lord Grey and his followers, who by their rash move had been separated from the main army and were surrounded by the enemy. Southampton and his troops had had to risk their lives as well, by charging through the dangerous bogs and did succeed in driving back the enemy, thus saving Lord Grey and his contingent.

Lord Grey was disciplined by being put under restraint for twenty-four hours and released. Humiliated by such treatment, he became a dangerous enemy to both Essex and Southampton. Grey's friends at Court (notably Cecil), long inimical to Essex and Southampton, seemed to have been successful in convincing the queen that Lord Grey had been misused and that Southampton had been high-handed. Whether Essex believed it was Elizabeth's directive that came by Cecil's letter it is unclear, but he defied the order and retained Southampton as General of the Horse. Together they continued winning more engagements against the rebels, while establishing their reputations as fearless and able leaders. Finally, on July 11, Essex wrote to the Privy Council asking them to cancel Southampton's dismissal. He brazenly accused the queen of only showing "dislike of his having any office." He was virtually denouncing the Privy Council, or perhaps Cecil, for "speaking for the Queen" and accusing them of duplicity. Though he may have been right, he was not being tactful or diplomatic:

> Was it treason in my Lord of Southampton to marry my poor kinswoman, that neither long imprisonment, nor no punishment besides that hath been usual in like cases, can satisfy or appease; or will no punishment be fit for him, but what punisheth not him, but me, this army, and this poor country of Ireland.[6]

If the queen had not been involved before, Essex's letter to the Council incensed her sufficiently to personally write him a stern rebuke and to express her amazement that he should:

> dare thus to value your own pleasing in things unnecessary, and think by your private arguments to carry for your own glory a matter wherein our pleasure to the contrary is made notorious.[7]

By August the English troops had a series of set-backs and some important losses. Cahir had been recaptured by the Irish, and the English had been caught in several ambushes by the rebels. Prospects were suddenly looking quite bleak for the English and particularly for Essex, who returned to Dublin in despair.

The queen was now complaining that Essex's long Leinster and Munster excursion had been unnecessary, even though she and the Privy Council had approved the plan in writing before Essex started out. Now she was heard to say that she had paid

£1000 a day for Essex "to go on a progresse."[8]

To make matters worse, Lord Grey had returned to London and the Court. How he managed to escape from his commitment in Ireland is not clear, but it could well have been Robert Cecil's doing. He could have been serving as a Cecil spy from the beginning of the campaign and then been called home when Cecil felt he was no longer needed in the field.

Cecil and Grey were busy at the Court giving every kind of bad report to the queen and the Privy Council. While they were pressing in the Privy Council for Essex to attack Tyrone in the north of Ireland, Essex was in a frenzy, knowing that he did not have the men or supplies to carry out the orders. Cecil seemed to be deliberately forcing Essex into an impossible situation. The queen now sent Essex an ultimatum to carry out the northern campaign against Tyrone and wrote him that:

> 'till the northern action be tried,' she was canceling his permission to return to England whenever he saw fit, for personal consultation with her Majesty.[9]

Essex was trapped, not by the enemy in Ireland but by his more subtle and more deadly enemies at Court. Cecil strongly influenced the aged queen's opinions and decisions. Robert Cecil had learned all the lessons of guile from his father, and if it was possible, he had learned to be even more self-serving and vicious. His brother-in-law, the earl of Oxford, must have recognized these characteristics in him even as a young man, for he used him as the model for Richard III. Cecil had effectively out-maneuvered Essex; he could neither attack Tyrone with an inadequate force nor could he return to England:

Bogged down hopelessly in Ireland, denied access to the Queen while his enemies flocked to her Court, Essex turned madly to thoughts of rebellion . . . in the latter part of August, Blount (Sir Christopher, Essex' step-father) was visited by Essex and Southampton. In 1601, after the failure of the "Essex Rebellion," Blount gave an account of what transpired at that meeting. Essex had announced his decision to sail for Wales with between 2,000 and 3,000 of his best troops. Landing at Milford Haven, he would be joined by other forces and march on London.[10]

Blount could not approve of the plan; his advice to Essex was more moderate. If he felt obliged to return to England, he should take with him only sufficient of his friends to protect him from his private enemies. Southampton reported later that he knew nothing of Essex's plan until the meeting with Blount, but that he too had "held it (the plan) altogether unfit."[11]

Akrigg finds no evidence of Southampton's frame of mind at this time but assumes that Southampton would have been angered by the queen cancelling his appointment as General of the Horse.

The situation at this point did not appear critical for either Essex or Southampton. After thinking things over, Essex gave up his wild ideas of rebellion. He then prepared to march north to Ulster and make some attempt to attack Tyrone.

On September 3, Essex finally found Tyrone, who seemed more interested in making a peace treaty than fighting a set battle against trained English troops; the Irish rebels were far better at sudden raids and ambushes. Essex was persuaded to meet with Tyrone in the middle of a stream for a private parley, and this turned out to be Essex's most important mistake.

At Essex's first meeting with Tyrone, on horseback in mid-stream, the Irishman asked Essex to join the rebellion with him against the queen, which, of course, he quickly refused. However, they did decide that a truce was mutually advantageous. Later, representatives from each side met to write a formal agreement:

> The rebels were to remain in possession of whatever they now held. No new garrison posts were to be set up. A very explicit time limit was set on the peace: it was to last by renewable six-week periods until May 1st. A provision for its termination at any time upon fourteen days notice played completely into Tyrone's hands. He was expecting an expeditionary force to arrive from Spain to assist him.[12]

Essex had now become ill with dysentery and retired to Drogheda to get medical help. In the meantime the report of the truce with Tyrone had reached England and the queen was furious. She felt, first of all, that the great expense of sending Essex and his army to Ireland was entirely wasted. But even more serious was the terrible threat to England if the Spaniards should successfully establish themselves in Ireland.

It seems as though Essex had not been thoroughly briefed on the real issues behind the campaign in Ireland, and it is difficult now to imagine the confusion that prevailed at every level of management in the government and the armed forces at that time. Communications were slow and the Council in London had no conception of the immediate concerns of the battlefield. Ill, Essex was in no state to think rationally or to command an army.

At this point, Elizabeth sent a final command to Essex not to pardon Tyrone nor to sign any formal pact with him until all proposals had been submitted to her in writing and until she had given her warrant in writing to proceed. This was a wise and reasonable executive decision, but Essex's response was rash and rebellious.

Assembling a group of his friends as a personal bodyguard, Essex embarked for England, leaving the earl of Ormonde, Anne Boleyn's Irish cousin, in charge of the English forces. Arriving in London, Essex and half a dozen followers mounted swift horses to race to Nonsuch, where the Queen was in residence. Lord Grey, having heard of Essex's return, had set out ahead of Essex:

> On the road Essex was overtaken by Sir Thomas Gerard. Gerard, aware that Grey was ahead, sped on and asked him (Grey) if he would not pull up and exchange greetings with his former commander. When Grey refused, alleging he had business at Court, Gerard frankly begged him to let Essex 'ride before, that he may bring the first newes of his return himself.' Grey asked if this request was made by Essex himself, to which Gerard made the spirited reply, No, nor I thincke will desire nothing at your hands.' At this Lord Grey resumed his dash towards Nonsuch.[13]

When Gerard reported his failure to Essex, one of his companions, Sir Christopher St. Lawrence, offered to ride after Grey, murder him, then find Cecil at Nonsuch and murder him, too. Essex refused the offer. This moment's decision on the road to Nonsuch was probably a major turning point in English history. Had Robert Cecil been murdered on that fateful day, Elizabeth would have been free to put her own son on the English throne, and the Tudors would never have experienced their "doom and date" of Sonnet 14. Arriving at Nonsuch just minutes after Lord Grey, Essex marched directly to the Royal apartments. Since Grey had gone in search of his mentor, Cecil, Essex beat him to the Royal Presence. Essex was convinced that all his troubles were due to his enemies at Court, the Cecil-Grey faction, and was sure that if he could see the queen alone, he could explain everything and regain her favor. Accordingly, Essex, liberally splashed with mud from his wild ride, burst into the astonished queen's presence in the midst of her toilette. The ubiquitous Rowland Whyte once again records the scene:

> . . . he kneeled unto her, kissed her hands, and had some privat speach with her, which seemed to give him great contentment; for coming from her Majesty to goe shifte himself in his chamber, he was very pleasant and thanked God, though he had suffered much Trouble and Storms Abroad, he found a sweet Calm at Home. 'Tis much wondred at here, that he went so boldly to her Majesty's Presence, she not being ready, and he soe full of Dirt and Mire, that his very face was full of yt. About 11 he was ready, and went up againe to the Queen, and conferred with her till half an Howre after 12. As yet all was well, and her Usage Very gracious towards hym. He went to Dinner, and during all that tyme, discoursed merely (entirely) of his Travels and Journeys in Ireland, of the goodnes of the Countrey, the Civilities of the Nobility that are true Subjects, of the great Intertainment he had in their Houses, of the good Orders he fownd there. He was visited frankly by all Sortes here of Lordes and Ladies, and Gentlemen.

> Only strangeness (coolness) is observed between hym and
> Mr. Secretary, and that Party . . . Then he went up to the
> Queen, but found her much changed in that small tyme,
> for she began to call hym to question for his return.[14]

Essex never again had a chance to speak with the queen.
There is no written record of who or what changed Elizabeth's
mind, but it had to be the work of Robert Cecil. By evening
Essex was ordered confined to his quarters. The following morning the Privy Council sat to consider the problem of Essex's
unauthorized return to England.

When they adjourned for dinner at noon, Court observers
were swift to mark how the division into two factions was sig-
naled by who dined with Cecil and who dined with Essex. Those
who went with Mr. Secretary were the earls of Shrewsbury and
Nottingham, Lord Thomas Howard, Lord Cobham, Lord Grey
and Sir George Carew. Those who went to Essex's table were
the earl of Worcester and the earl of Rutland, Lord Mountjoy,
Lord Rich, Lord Henry Howard, Lord Lumley and a number
of knights.[15]

According to the above list of adversaries, there were more
in sympathy with Essex than against him. At two o'clock the
Privy Council reconvened and required Essex to answer to six
charges, most of which seemed forced issues. Cecil was evidently
doing his utmost to build a mountain out of a bit less than a
molehill.

The issues were:

(1) His contemptuous disobedience to Her Majesty's instructions in returning to England.

Since this was an edict probably originating in Cecil's fer-
tile brain and subsequently transformed by guile to the queen's

"Order," this is not as serious as Cecil makes it seem. The queen's graciousness and her genuine pleasure in seeing Essex on his return seems to indicate that she had not given that particular command.

(2) His presumptuous letters written from time to time.

Essex had always been brash with the queen and had often taken liberties that would have ruined others. This was a personal Cecil complaint, not the queen's, and therefore this was unwarranted.

(3) His proceedings in Ireland contrary to the course agreed upon in England before he went there.

This was a specious charge since Essex had written a full report to the queen and the Privy Council, and they, in turn, had sent him written instructions to proceed with his alternate plan as proposed.

(4) His rash manner in coming away from Ireland.

This is really a repeat of the number one charge and therefore simply redundant.

(5) His overbold intrusion the previous day into Her Majesty's bed chamber.

Since Her Majesty had not been angered by the sudden intrusion, Cecil's concern seems overzealous. Essex's precipitate behavior on this occasion is perhaps one proof that he was on sufficiently casual terms with the queen to feel free to walk into her chambers. It also shows how desperate Essex felt about reaching the Queen before Cecil could interfere.

(6) His creation of an inordinate number of knights (more than seventy) while in Ireland.

This may have been a serious lapse of judgment on Essex's part, but it hardly seems relevant to the inquiry and without more information on the particular circumstances of how, when, and why these honors were given out, it is impossible to assess his actions. Yet this, too, seems to have been another piece of Cecil's constructed mountain:

> After Essex left, the Privy Councillors talked things over for fifteen minutes and then went to the Queen to deliver their verdict. Elizabeth took a day to think things over. Then, on Monday, October 1st, she announced her verdict. She had decided against Essex.[16]

This account omits the Council's verdict, nor does it tell who reported it to the queen or who returned the Queen's verdict to the Privy Council. It sounds as though the Queen had not been there in person. Earlier, the queen had met with the Privy Council in London to make decisions about Ireland, but in this instance it sounds as though she were distanced from the hearing. Cecil seems to be controlling the Council and perhaps even the Queen.

Essex was taken from Nonsuch to London to be held prisoner at York House, the Lord Keeper's residence. There Essex became increasingly morbid and again ill. Not long after, the Queen (or Cecil) had Sir Christopher St. Lawrence and others who had accompanied Essex sent back to Ireland. Lord Mountjoy, who had sat with the Essex faction at dinner on the fateful day at Nonsuch, was sent to Ireland as the new Lord Deputy. With everything resolved the Privy Council asked the queen to release Essex, but she (or Cecil) refused the request:

> We come now to the problem as to why, month after month, Elizabeth kept the hapless Earl, miserably ill and

unconvicted by any court, the prisoner of an increasingly impatient Lord Keeper Egerton. Essex's friends declared that it was all Cecil's doing. They pictured the little hunchback as a malevolent Machiavellian, inspired by hateful jealousy for the magnificent Essex.[17]

Later, in James I reign, Robert Prickett composed a doggerel that spoke for the Essexian view of Cecil:

> Then in that time an undermining wit,
> Did closely frame all actions jumply fit,
> Molehills were to mountain raisde,
> Each little fault was much dispraisde.
> [...]
> Herein lay the secret ill,
> She sought to chide, they sought to kill.[18]

Essex was no match for the wily Cecil in a power play, for the latter had learned every underhanded stratagem from his father and then devised a few of his own. Burghley had quite literally climbed over the dead bodies of hundreds who had trusted him and who were then betrayed by him to reach his pinnacle of power and wealth.[19] His son Robert was handed the power and wealth like a baton in a relay race but seemed to have an even more vicious appetite than his father. Determined to destroy Essex and the entire Essex faction, he planned every move with care and villainous guile.

Essex was next threatened with a Star Chamber inquiry, which was undoubtedly Cecil's maneuver, but it was finally cancelled (perhaps by the Queen). On hearing that it had been cancelled, Essex's mother, Lettice Knollys Blount, the earl of

Southampton, and some other close friends gained access to a house that overlooked York House and exchanged greetings with Essex. "This maneuver was not well received at Court," according to Professor Akrigg in his biography of Southampton. This may mean that it was Cecil reacting again and not the queen.

In March of 1600, Essex was released from York house and sent to his own home. However, he remained in custody and all his friends and relatives sent elsewhere. Cecil was taking no chances. Southampton, meanwhile, tried to make peace with the queen but was not permitted to see her. The hand of Cecil seems to have been controlling Southampton as well as Essex.

The animosity between Lord Grey and Southampton had been building while Essex was undergoing his ordeal, and this led eventually to a duel on the continent. There has been some question whether the duel actually took place, because they had both received an order from the Queen forbidding them to fight. Southampton's biographer, Charlotte Stopes, notes that "though Southampton and Grey fought, no wounds seem to have been received on either side." Akrigg, however, feels that "there is a strong possibility that Southampton was seriously hurt in the duel. When Rowland Whyte reported to Robert Sidney that the earl of Southampton had returned to England, he noted "he hath been extreme sicke, but is now recovered."[20]

Akrigg suggests that the "extreme sicke" was in all likelihood a fiction invented to account for the period when Southampton was recovering from his wounds and for his subsequent wan appearance. A footnote elucidation of the last statement is vitally important:

The friends of both Southampton and Lord Grey would of course be busy denying that they had duelled in defiance of the Queen's orders. One who seems to have been persuaded by their disavowals is John Chamberlain, who on October 12th belatedly reported, 'The erle of Southampton and the Lord Gray are come out of the Lowe Countries unhurt, though it was constantly reported they had fought and spoyled (wounded) each other' (Letters I, 107). Presumably Cecil, who as Secretary would have opened Grey's panicky letter confessing disobedience, had done him (Southampton) the kindness of suppressing its contents.[21]

Grey's letter to the Privy Council had indeed been a confession. "May it please your Lordships: I assure my self yow either are, or will shortly bee infourmed of my disobedience..."[22]

Cecil's interception of this letter was done to save his friend and ally Lord Grey. It was certainly not done in Southampton's interest. It is more likely that Cecil may have encouraged, or even ordered, Grey to challenge Southampton and if possible to kill him. Southampton, by his very existence, was the biggest threat to Cecil's future. Should Southampton succeed Elizabeth, Cecil would be in jeopardy; perhaps his very life depended on it. If Southampton were to become king, Cecil would surely be called before the Star Chamber to answer for his treasonable behavior to Southampton and his friends, particularly Essex. For Cecil it was almost a choice of kill or be killed. Since neither Southampton or Essex were as vicious as Cecil, it was an uneven conflict.

In September, Southampton, back in England and recovered from his wounds, met with Essex, who had been released from house arrest and was tormented by worry over his finances. Since Essex's father had left him too small an estate to support his title, he had been almost wholly dependent on the queen's largesse. Considering Elizabeth's reputation for parsimony, she had been quite generous with Essex, and for a number of years he had had the "farm" of the duties on sweet wines imported from abroad. Leicester may have arranged for this originally, but renewal of the benefit was coming up at the end of September, and if it were discontinued, Essex would be virtually bankrupt.

Essex sent submissive and humble letters to the queen hoping to ingratiate himself, but he received no replies. Finally, at the end of October Elizabeth wrote to inform him that she had refused to renew his grant. At this time Elizabeth is reported to have remarked to Francis Bacon, Cecil's cousin and cohort in prosecuting Essex later:

> Essex has written me some dutiful letters, which moved me, but after taking them to flow from the abundance of his heart, I find them but a preparative to a suit for renewing his farm of sweet wines.[23]

Essex assumed that his enemies had been poisoning the queen's mind while he was still forbidden to attend Court. Undoubtedly Cecil was using all his guile and influence to eliminate Essex as a power at Court. Cecil had played his hand well and won; his subtle machinations had proved more effective than Essex's direct, impetuous honesty. It was Essex's rash, headlong action that was his final destruction and at the same time the undoing of his loyal friends and relatives. Sir John Harrington, the queen's godson, wrote of an interview he had with Essex at this time:

> ...he uttered strange words borderinge on such strange
> desyns, that made me hasten forthe and leave his
> presence...His speeches of the Queen becometh no man
> who hath 'mens sana in corpore sano.'[24]

Essex was ready to destroy himself and his loyal friends.
Cecil had only to sit back and let it happen. History would record
that Essex and Southampton were overambitious, overbold, and
traitorous, while Cecil, who manipulated them like puppets,
would receive accolades as the wise and faithful servant of the
queen.

In December of 1600 Essex House was in a turmoil of
preparation. Anti-Cecil feeling was running high, and Essex,
always popular among the common citizens as well as the nobility and gentry, was surrounded by supporters who hated and
feared Cecil. Both Essex and Southampton, as well as their many
supporters, endlessly protested that their rebellion was aimed
at removing Robert Cecil from power, not at the queen. They
were sure that if they could reach the queen, they could wrest
control from Cecil, and Cecil himself must have felt this to be
true. After Essex's one successful intrusion at Nonsuch and
Elizabeth's friendly response, Cecil must have known that the
only way he could maintain his control over the queen was to
keep both Essex and Southampton away from her. She was genuinely fond of Essex, who was not only a "favorite" but a close
relative, for he was the grandson of her first cousin, or great-
grandson of her aunt, Mary Boleyn Carey. She also had a strong
natural attachment to her own son, Southampton, though he
had given her much cause for distress as a "problem child" at

Court.

Cecil's clever manipulations succeeded in keeping Elizabeth's close relatives from her presence at this critical time. As Secretary he had a decided advantage in screening all correspondence and appointments. Also, he had inherited a vast and efficient spy network from his father. Essex complained that his every word and his every move were reported immediately to Cecil during his confinement to Essex House.

One maneuver in Essex's preparations was an attempt to enlist the aid of the Scottish King, James VI.

On Christmas Day, 1600, Essex dispatched to King James a long detailed letter which he had drafted with the aid of Southampton, Sir Charles Danvers, and Henry Cuffe. It is a very significant document. In it Essex enumerates all the wrongs that Cecil and his faction have done against him: they have corrupted servants of his, stolen papers belonging to him, suborned false witnesses, and employed forged documents against him. They have sought to suppress "all noble, virtuous, and heroical spirits." They have conspired with the Spanish Infanta and have made "devilish plots with your Majesty's own subjects against your person and your life."[25]

Then Essex announces that he will wrest control of the government from these monsters:

> Now am I summoned of all sides to stop the malice, the wickedness and madness of these men, and to relieve my poor country that groans under her burthen. Now doth reason, honor, and conscience command me to be active. Now do I see by God's favor the fairest and likeliest hope that it can be of good success.[26]

A week prior to sending for help from King James, Essex and his friends had been concerned by a Court rumor that Southampton was to be arrested. However, Cecil had evidently not been successful in arranging it, for the arrest did not materialize. Soon after this Cecil resorted to more violent means of eliminating the earl.

On January 9, 1601, Southampton, accompanied only by his horseboy, was riding in the vicinity of Ralegh's residence and was viciously attacked by Lord Grey and a band of his followers. Southampton held off the attackers until help arrived, but his boy had one of his hands lopped off. The queen swiftly punished Lord Grey, committing him to the Fleet Prison, but in Essex House a new fantasy crowded into the fevered minds of Essex and his coterie—their enemies, afraid to proceed against them by due course of law, were out to murder them. When Grey was given his release on February 2, Essex, Southampton, and their friends took it as proof that the law would no longer protect them.[27]

This murderous attack was scarcely "a fantasy of fevered minds," but the calculated move of the diabolical Cecil. The attack on Southampton indicates several things: Cecil was fearful that Henry Wriothesley, earl of Southampton, would succeed his mother, the queen, to the throne when she died. Being of a ruthless nature himself, Cecil must have assumed that his enemies would, when they came to power, deal with him as viciously as he would himself were he in their position. The queen was aging and obviously nearing her end. Therefore, if Cecil did not succeed in eliminating the Tudor heir by some means within a short time, the queen's death could spell Cecil's own doom.

The attack on Southampton also shows that Cecil took the Essex faction seriously. As mentioned before, Essex was extremely popular with almost everyone, nobility and commoners alike. Cecil was, on the other hand, feared and hated. He and his father reinstituted cruel medieval tortures of the many unfortunate souls whom they chose to interrogate. Cecil's cousin and close associate, Francis Bacon, was said by the queen to have "the eye of a viper." Lord Grey, Cecil's close ally, was violent and murderous. These were the unsavory characters who were momentarily at the center of power and were determined to stay there.

Another important point to notice in the account of Grey's attack on Southampton is the remarkable speed with which Grey regained his freedom. This had to be the work of Cecil, who probably gave the order for the assault, and, as quickly as he dared, gave the order for the release of the perpetrator.

If Essex felt any complacency at the progress of his preparations, that complacency ended on Saturday, February 7. On that day, the government, alerted by its informers, sent John Herbert, the second Secretary of State, to Essex House with a summons for Essex to attend forthwith a meeting of the Privy Council at which he would be instructed how to conduct himself. Essex, fearing imprisonment, refused to leave Essex House, making an excuse that ill health kept him from attending.[28]

That evening Essex held a consultation with his sister, Lady Rich; his step-father, Sir Christopher Blount; one of his cousins, Sir Robert Vernon; Sir Charles Danvers, and Southampton. Now that Cecil had taken the initiative, Essex was uncertain how to act. Danvers advised him "To fly with some hundred gentle men to the sea side, or into Wales, where he might command some ports."[29]

Unfortunately, Essex had received word by his secretary that he could be assured of support in the city of London, apparently from Sheriff Smith, who had a thousand men of the London militia under his command. Convinced that the city of London would support his cause, Essex decided not to flee. Before dawn on February 8, messengers were out summoning supporters of the rebellion to Essex House. While the company was assembling, a message arrived from Sir Walter Ralegh, Captain of the Queen's Guard, that he wanted Sir Ferdinando Gorges to come over to talk with him. Essex insisted that Gorges go out in a boat to meet Ralegh "on the water upon equal terms."[30]

When Gorges returned, he reported that Ralegh had tried to persuade him that he would be ruined if he remained at Essex House but that he had rejected Ralegh's warning. Subsequent testimony at Essex's trial would reveal that Gorges had, in reality, disclosed Essex's plans to arm his friends and proceed to the city. Essex, being guileless and honest himself, was too ready to trust others. He would be betrayed repeatedly in the critical days ahead and deserted by those he had counted on.

Later that morning four emissaries from the Court arrived at Essex House, Sir Thomas Egerton, Essex's recent warder at York House; Sir William Knollys, Essex's uncle; Lord Chief Justice Popham, and the earl of Worcester. When these four announced that the queen had sent them to determine the reasons for Essex's discontent and why he had thus assembled these men, Essex replied in a very loud voice "that his life was sought, and that he should have been murdered in his bed."[31]

When these Privy Council members promised that Essex should receive a full hearing and justice, Southampton interrupted to remind them that he himself had already been attacked by Lord Grey, a council member. Chief Justice Popham replied that Grey had been punished and then tried to persuade them to enter the house for a private conference. At that the crowd of several hundred supporters in the courtyard made a great outcry, warning Essex: "Away, my Lord! They abuse you! They betray you! They undo you! You lose time!"[32]

At this the Lord Keeper, who had removed his hat in deference to Essex, now put his hat on to indicate that he was speaking for the queen and commanded them all on their allegiance to the queen to lay down their weapons and depart. Without a word Essex marched into the house, and the four emissaries followed while the crowd shouted, "Kill them!"[33] On reaching a room at the back of the house and following the suggestions of Southampton, Blount, and Danvers, Essex gave orders to have the four men locked up there. Essex left Danvers to watch over the prisoners along with an armed guard commanded by Owen Salisbury.[34]

If Essex had had the efficient spy system at his command that Robert Cecil had, he would have known that the queen was at Whitehall, just a short distance from Essex House. He would have known, too, that she had only the palace guard to protect her. Essex, with his band of friends and troops of supporters, could have reached Elizabeth with little difficulty. Essex and Southampton had repeatedly insisted that their aim was to talk personally with her because they were sure that she would listen to their complaints and protect them from their enemies. They were sure this was the only way that they could escape their assassins.

A few days after this day of crisis, Master Vincent Hussey wrote of Essex:

> It is a blessed thing that he failed in Judgement and attempted London first, for had he gone straight to Court, he would have surprised it *unprovided of defence*, and *full of well-wishers*, before the world had notice of his treasons.[35]

William Camden, who was authorized by the Cecils to write the official history of Elizabeth's reign (and who was provided with the Cecil's own records from which he wrote a distinctly biased view of history) reports, "...the rebels lacked arms and believed the guard at Whitehall had been doubled." While Cecil was obtaining accurate and complete information from his numerous spies, he was evidently feeding the Essex faction some important misinformation.

Essex had originally planned to arrive at St. Paul's Church in time to address the crowds assembled for Sunday service, but the meeting with the queen's emissaries had delayed him and he was too late. In the meantime Cecil's troops were closing off the city with chains and barricades. Essex, Southampton, and their followers, armed only with swords and daggers, finally arrived at Sheriff Smith's house in Fenchurch Street.

> Smith seems to have played for time. While her servants provided Essex's followers with beer, he headed off to the Lord Mayor with Essex's request that he come to him . . . While Essex was achieving little or nothing at Sheriff Smith's house, word came that Robert Cecil's brother, Lord Burghley (the second Lord Burghley) was at hand with a

herald and a dozen horsemen. Despite Lord Monteagle's frantic orders to stop the herald's throat, Garter King at Arms read the Queen's proclamation declaring Essex a traitor.[36]

Although Monteagle's men finally drove Burghley, the herald, and their guard away, the damage was done:

> Essex desperately tried to rally his followers, declaring this was a trick played by his enemies, that for two shillings a herald would say anything, and that it was he, Essex, who stood for the good of the Queen and of London.[37]

It seemed as though Robert Cecil were in charge of all actions and that the queen did not really know what was going on and may have been fed lies by Cecil for a long time before the "rebellion." Cecil did much the same thing to James I when he came to the throne, for he played on James' fears constantly in order to make himself indispensable to the King. The most famous ruse of this sort was the Guy Fawkes Gunpowder plot, shown in recent years to have originated with Robert Cecil.[38]

Essex's followers lost courage on hearing the herald's proclamation and faded away, slipping out of sight down side streets, and the Londoners stolidly refused to join in. Fear of Cecil and the label of treason was too intimidating. However, Essex, with his shrinking forces, headed westward rather aimlessly not knowing quite where to go or what to do:

> At two in the afternoon the rebels arrived at Ludgate, where the Earl of Cumberland had posted a company of pikemen and halberdiers under the command of Sir John

Levenson. At Essex's approach, Levenson adamantly refused to withdraw the chain set across the road. Sir Ferdinand Gorges, after fruitless attempts to negotiate with Levenson, asked Essex to let him release his hostages and travel with them to Whitehall, there to secure the best terms he could before any blood was shed. Essex saw some merit in the plan but sent off Gorges with authority to release only one of his hostages, Chief Justice Popham.[39]

Sir John Levenson gave his own account later of what happened next:

> One of the Earl's side cried, 'Shoot, shoot!' and then the pistols were discharged at us within a three-quarters pike's length of us, and they were answered again by such shot as we had, and forthwith Sir Christopher Blount charged with his sword and target and came close to the chain and cut off the head of sundry the pikes, and with him divers others of the Earl's company, of which some got between the post and the chain and let drive among our pikes and halberds; and in this encounter Sir Chr. Blount was hurt, first by a thrust in the face, and then felled by a knock on the head. Upon the sight whereof and the fall of young Mr. Tracy, the Earl's page, our company coming upon them put them back, which the Earl perceiving called them off and so departed from us.[40]

Levenson's second-in-command was killed in the encounter, and Essex was narrowly missed by two bullets that went through his hat. Essex and his dwindling band of followers retired to the river, where boats were found for the leaders. Essex and Southampton should have headed downstream and made their escape to the continent. The opportunity was there, but Essex still believed that he could negotiate with the queen by holding his remaining hostages prisoners. On landing at the water stairs at Essex House, he found that Gorges had left fifteen minutes earlier with all four of the hostages.

Retiring into the house, Essex found that the place was surrounded and began burning papers that he felt might incriminate him. Soon Lord Burghley led an assault on Essex House, broke down the gates, and took possession of the courtyard, losing two of his men in the foray. Among the defenders, Southampton lost one of his footmen, and Owen Salisbury was mortally wounded. While this was going on, artillery was being brought from the Tower. With the artillery in place, they held their fire while the Lord Admiral sent Sir Robert Sidney, a long-time friend of Essex and his associates, to persuade them to surrender peacefully. Southampton stepped out on the roof to reply to this proposal:

> Insisting that Essex and the rest of them had taken up arms only to defend themselves from their enemies, and that they meant no harm to the Queen, Southampton said that they were ready to present themselves before her Majesty if the Lord Admiral would give hostages to guarantee their safe return. Sidney's reply was that subjects must not seek to bargain with Princes, and he reminded Southampton that Essex House was not so strongly built that it could hold out against the Lord Admiral's cannon. To this Southampton retorted that the rebels would rather die like men, with swords in their hands, than end their lives in ten days time on the scaffold. Essex had by now joined Southampton on the roof. He declared that he

would have done God and his country good service by rooting out from England those 'Atheists and Caterpillars' who were their enemies. He said that he shared Southampton's resolution to die and accounted it the greatest punishment that God had ever laid on him that he had not suffered him to die during his sickness of the previous year.[41]

Then the Lord Admiral declared a truce to allow time for the women to evacuate Essex House. During this time the rebels argued whether they should fight to the end and die "with honor" or give up and hope for mercy. Finally they announced from the roof top that they would surrender on three conditions. First, the Lord Admiral must give civil treatment to Essex and his followers; second, they must all have a fair and impartial trial; and third, Essex must be allowed the spiritual ministrations of Ashton, a clergyman in whom he had great trust.

The Lord Admiral accepted these conditions and the doors of Essex House were opened. Essex, Southampton, and all their followers, on their knees, handed over their swords to Lord Admiral Nottingham.[42] At ten o'clock in the evening the "rebellion" was over. Their day had begun before dawn with the message from Sir Walter Ralegh and now eighteen hours later, Essex and Southampton were led away as prisoners, hoping for fair play but not likely to receive it. The news was quickly relayed to the queen, who had refused to sleep until she knew the outcome of the day's events.

Akrigg reports that, "The authorities dared not lead their prisoners through the streets to the Tower that night for fear of demonstrations on the way." This seems to show the popularity and support for Essex and Southampton and at the same time indicates the extent of fear and hatred for Cecil among the people. The prisoners were, therefore, lodged at first with the Archbishop of Canterbury in Lambeth.

The order soon came, however, that they must be taken to the Tower. It is not clear who gave the order, but since Elizabeth had retired for the night, it must have been Cecil who assumed that responsibility. He had been subtly aiming for this outcome for a long time and must have felt triumphant that night. At three in the morning of February 9, a little less than twenty-four hours after the start of the whole operation, Essex, Southampton, and their main supporters were transferred to the Tower. From there that night Southampton wrote a letter to his wife:

> Sweet hart I doute not but you shall heare ere I come to you of the misfortune of your friends, bee not to(o) apprehensive of it, for gods will must be donn, & what is allotted to us by destiny cannot bee avoyded; beleeve that in this time there is nothing can so much comfort mee as to thinke you are well & take patiently what hath happened, & contrariwise I shall live in torment if I find you vexed for my cause, doubt not but I shall doe well & please your self with the assurance that I shall ever remayn
> your affectionat husband
> H. Southampton[43]

A footnote in Professor Akrigg's biography of Southampton makes the observation:

> The letter was addressed simply, "To my Bess." Miss Tennison is probably right when she thought that, since the letter ended up in the Cecil archives, it was probably

never delivered to the wife.[44]

Robert Cecil was taking no chances. His enemies must be held incommunicado, and his suspicious nature could not allow a simple note of affection to reach a distraught wife.

Akrigg writes:

> London now had the appearance of an armed camp. Troops were deployed about the city. One of Essex's captains, Thomas Lee, was reported to be plotting to seize the Queen and force her to sign a warrant for the Earl's release.[45]

This may have been another one of the "planted plots" Cecil used to keep Elizabeth, and later James I, in a state of panic and entirely dependent on him. Whether the report was true or not, Lee was arrested and joined the other ninety of Essex's followers already in the Tower, Newgate, Marshalsea, and several other of the dreadful prisons in London.

> When, one week after the failure of the rebellion, Londoners came to St. Paul's Cross for the Sunday sermon and the preacher (carefully briefed by the government) launched into denunciations of Essex, five hundred armed men stood by in case the sermon provoked demonstrations on Essex's behalf.[46]

> The queen's ministers (or Cecil) moved quickly to bring the leaders of the revolt to trial. Letters were sent (by Cecil) to the peers selected to hear the case (a jury hand-picked by Cecil).[47]

Unbelievably and brazenly, Cecil chose the murderous Lord Grey to sit in judgment on a man he had tried to kill in a duel, and failing that, to assassinate in the streets of London and for which he had been punished with a scant three weeks in jail. The letters promised the Lords that they:

> shall be further acquainted with all the peculiarities not only of their (Essex and Southampton) secret practises of treason againste this kingdom but of their actuall rebellion within the citty of London, where they assembled great forces on Sunday laste and killed divers of her Majesty's subjects.[48]

Cecil was taking no chances with the verdict. Instead of the fair and impartial trial promised by the Lord Admiral, Cecil was making sure that the jury would pre-judge the defendants. Though the Attorney-General, Sir Edward Coke, took pains to protest that no torture had been used, or even threatened, two of the conspirators, Sir John Davies and Sir Ferdinando Gorges, were ready to testify. (It seems that if torture had not been used, it would have been unnecessary to deny it.) The trial was held on February 19th. Such a brief hearing has the appearance of a mere formality:

> The two Earls, under heavy guard, were brought up the river in barges to Westminster Hall. It was almost nine o'clock in the morning when the Lord High Steward preceded by seven sergeant-at-arms bearing maces, entered the court and took his place in a high canopied chair. Garter King of Arms stood on one side of him, and a gentleman usher, carrying a white rod of office, stood on the

other. Sir Walter Ralegh, Captain of the Queen's Guard, and forty of his yeomen were also present.[49]

The two prisoners were then brought in, preceded by a gentleman porter carrying an axe with the blade turned away from the defendants. Essex appeared cheerful and confident, but Southampton seemed somewhat sad. The Attorney General then stated the court's case:

> He that raiseth power and strength in a settled government the law doeth construe it highe treason. He that doe usurpe upon it, the law doeth intend that he purposeth the destruction of the Prince. He that assembles powers, if the Kinge doth command him uppon his allegiaunce to desolve his company, and he contineweth it without any question it is highe treason.[50]

Coke then continued in a less formal vein to scold Essex for his ingratitude for all the favors that the queen had bestowed on him. Then turning to Southampton, he rebuked hm for being ungrateful for all the queen's benefits, even though his misconduct at Court had caused her distress. Coke also accused Essex of having been determined to be Robert the First of England.

Essex, protesting, replied, "Mr. Attorney playeth the orator and abuseth your Lordships' ears with slanders against us. These are the fashions of orators in corrupt states, and such rhetoric is the trade and talent of those who value themselves upon their skill in pleading innocent men out of their lives."[51]

The prosecution's evidence was then presented, which mostly consisted of reading confessions obtained from prisoners by officers of the Crown. It is a known fact that both Lord Burghley and his son Robert after him were more than efficient at getting "confessions" when needed. They made a practice of always being present at "interrogations" to make certain that the "questioners" were doing a proper job, and they never failed to get the desired results.

Essex, after hearing a reading of Gorges' confession and probably aware of these methods, asked to confront him face to face. Gorges was then brought to court to answer Essex's questions. One bit of information from this confrontation brought Cecil out of hiding:

> To justify the declarations he had made on the day of the rebellion that a plot existed to let the Spanish Infanta inherit the English crown, Essex testified that he had been told by a member of the Privy Council that Sir Robert Cecil himself had informed him that the Infanta's claim to the succession was as good as any other's.[52]

At this point Robert Cecil, who interestingly had chosen the same "cover" as Polonius in *Hamlet* , stepped from behind the arras to refute the charge. In what seems like a prepared speech, he glorified himself in comparison to Essex with a string of blatant untruths:

> My Lord of Essex, the difference between you and me is great. For wit I give you the pre-eminence—you have it abundantly. For nobility also I give you place—I am not noble, yet a gentleman; I am no swordsman-there also you have the odds; but I have innocence, conscience, truth and honesty to defend me against the scandal and sting of slan-

derous tongues, and in this Court I stand as an upright man, and your Lordship as a delinquent. I protest before God, I have loved your person and justified your virtues: and I appeal to God and the Queen, that I told her Majesty your afflictions would make you a fit servant for her, attending but a fit time to move Her Majesty to call you to the Court again. And had I not seen your ambitious affections inclined toward usurpation, I would have gone on my knees to her Majesty to have done you good; but you have a wolf's head in a sheep's garment...Ah, my Lord, were it but your own case, the loss had been less; but you have drawn a number of noble persons and gentlemen of birth and quality into your net of rebellion, and their bloods will cry vengeance against you. For my part, I vow to God, I wish my soul had been in heaven and my body at rest that this had not been.[53]

Cecil, demanding to know the source of the statement about the Infanta, could get no answer from Essex but managed to persuade Southampton that "it were fit" that he disclose the originator of this statement. Southampton finally told him that it was Essex's uncle, Sir William Knollys.

Knollys was soon brought into the court but denied that Cecil had ever made the claim and protested that he had been referring to a seditious book by a Jesuit, Robert Parsons, in which he said that the Infanta had a valid claim to the throne. History does not tell us if Knollys recanted out of fear of Cecil, but chances are this was the reason.

After this encounter there was nothing more that could be said. It would have been impossible at that point to claim that Southampton was the legitimate heir to the Throne. Until and unless the queen was ready to proclaim his rights, Southampton could say nothing without seeming to prove that the rebellion was indeed a move to usurp the Crown.

However, Essex did make one last attempt with a plea that "Man is governed by three laws: Nature, Reason, and God, and that his own action had been according to the law of Nature, self-preservation, since he had known that his enemies were out to destroy him." He insisted once more that he had intended nothing against the queen and had sought access to her only to present his case.[54]

Essex knew before it was over that he had lost, and he talked bravely of going to his death with courage, but Southampton was not ready to give up. Coke had accused him of being one of a group of Catholic malcontents, and this Southampton vigorously denied:

> And where as you charge me to be a Papist I protest most unfainedly that I was never conversant with any of that sort only I knew one Wilde a priest of that sort that went up and dowen the towen but I niver conversed with him in all my lief.[55]

Southampton also denied the charge from the earl of Rutland's testimony that he had long been discontented and had stirred up Essex to his rebellion. He insisted, too, that he had not known until he arrived at Essex House Sunday morning that Essex was planning to march on London.

Pleading was in vain; the verdict had been decided before the two earls had entered the court. The Lord High Steward read the terrible sentence required by the law in the case of treason; they were to be hanged, drawn, and quartered . . . "and so God have mercy on your souls." The guard then led Essex and Southampton back to the Tower, the Gentleman Porter now carrying his axe with the blade turned towards the two condemned earls.[56]

Two days later Lord Treasurer Buckhurst, Lord Keeper Egerton, Lord Admiral Nottingham, and Secretary Cecil visited Essex in the Tower. Essex made a confession to these men, admitting that he and his associates had intended to force their way into the queen's presence to "use her authority to change the government and call a parliament, condemning their opponents for misgoverning the state."[57]

Essex also provided his visitors with names of his chief persuaders to "this great offence," his step-father, Sir Christopher Blount (who in actuality tried constantly to restrain his rash step-son); the earl's secretaries, Cuffe and Temple, and those who participated in the conferences. According to Cecil, at the end of the interview Essex asked that he be allowed to die privately and that the manner of execution be changed to beheading. The accuracy of this account is dubious and no written confession was preserved. Though Cecil claimed that Essex had asked for this interview, it is more likely that it was Cecil's idea. Cecil may well have used the offer of an easier death as a bargaining device to make Essex provides names of other "victims" for his murderous appetite. Cecil's letter to Lord Mountjoy in Ireland is the only source of this information, and the Cecils, father and son, always arranged to have the written record show the Cecils only as the wise and devoted servants of the Crown. Both father and son destroyed a vast number of state records during Queen Elizabeth's reign, preserving only those that showed the Cecils in a favorable light.

The real account of this meeting with Essex was probably quite different. Cecil probably did use guile to loosen Essex's tongue. With the threat of the tortured form of public execution already before Essex, it may have been a sufficient lure to implicate others. It is unfortunate if this was true, that Essex, to save himself a horrible death, allowed a number of other people to suffer in his place. Sir Gelly Merrick, his steward, and Henry Cuffe, his secretary, were taken to Tyburn and put through the dreadful process of being hanged, drawn, and quartered - a barbarous punishment. Also condemned to a beheading by Essex's "confession" were Sir Christopher Blount, Essex's second step-father, and Sir Charles Danvers. Earlier Danvers had declared:

> The principle motive that drove (him) into this action was the great obligation of love and duty, in respect of many honourable favours done to him by the Earl of Southampton. [58]

Southampton had several years earlier helped Sir Charles Danvers and his brother escape to the continent when they were in jeopardy. Now he had to pay in full his debt to Southampton. Southampton, in the meantime, waited in the Tower. His wife, Elizabeth Vernon Wriothesley, wrote abjectly to Robert Cecil to spare her husband:

> . . . Oh! let me, beseech you, in this my great distress move you to compassion . . . I restlessly remain the most
> unhappy and miserable
> Elizabeth Southampton [59]

It is interesting that the letter is addressed to Cecil, not the queen. It is telling, too, that she asks Cecil to have compassion, a curious plea unless it is one more proof of the extraordinary power that Cecil wielded at this point.

The queen, however, did succeed in saving her son from the scaffold, though she was unable to release him from the Tower. Possibly Cecil felt that Essex was more of a troublemaker than Southampton. With Essex out of the way Southampton was no longer a threat, as long as he was locked up in the Tower. With the Tudor heir safely put away, Cecil was then free to arrange the succession to suit his best interests. Or perhaps Cecil felt Southampton was more useful as a hostage to guarantee that there would be no uprisings of his supporters anxious to see the Tudor line perpetuated.

Whatever his p rpose, Cecil had his own way and continued to control the queen and the succession. The earl of Oxford, who had been obliged to sit on the judicial panel at the trial of his son, watched helplessly as his son was destroyed. He expressed his grief in exquisite sonnets addressed to his doomed son:; numbers 52, 55, 60, 64, 65, 67, 81, 100, 101, and 116 all express his anguish while he waited for the axe to fall. Of these perhaps number 116 is the most familiar and most loved:

> Let me not to the marriage of true minds
> Admit impediments. Love is not love
> Which alters when it alteration finds
> Or bends with the remover to remove.
> O, no! It is an ever fixéd mark
> That looks on tempests and is never shaken;
> It is the star to every wand'ring bark,
> Whose worth's unknown, although his height be taken.

Love's not time's fool, though rosy lips and cheeks
Within his bending sickle's compass come.
Love alters not with the brief hours and weeks,
But bears it out even to the edge of doom.
   If this be error, and upon me proved,
   I never writ, nor no man ever loved.

"True minds" are Vere minds. Oxford, obliged to sit in judgment on his own son, is telling Southampton that it looks as though his love for his son was altered and that he was "bending" with Cecil (just as Cecil was bent with deformity) by giving in to Cecil's "removal" of Southampton. Yet, in the next line with "O" representing Oxford and the negative following, he denies that he is bending with Cecil and playing the villain. Instead he is "ever" or E. Vere, Southampton's "fixéd mark" (as a mariner's Pole star, or guide, and the star on the de Vere escutcheon). He promises to be the star to guide E. Vere's wandering bark (ship), which is Southampton. His worth, or value as the Tudor heir, is unknown, even though "his height be taken," meaning that he has been bested by Cecil and laid low. Neither time nor the doom that Cecil had devised for Southampton will alter Oxford's love.

In the final couplet, he vows that this is only an error if "I never writ". "Nor no man ever loved" added to the first gives two avowals, which by negative proof guarantee the proof of his previous statements, for he wrote voluminously, and the second needs no comment except that E. Vere almost signs his name in the penultimate word "ever" and it is certain that he adored his Royal son.

9 ✳ BARE RUINED CHOIRS

QUEEN ELIZABETH'S HEALTH deteriorated steadily after the "Essex Rebellion," and it is commonly believed that her decline was due to remorse for executing Essex. It is true that she had fairly doted on her dashing great-nephew and had shown a surprising tolerance for his repeated offences. Romantic stories persist of Essex making a last minute appeal to the queen for a reprieve by sending her a ring she had given him, though she actually never received a message.

A story of unknown origin claims that Essex did indeed hand the ring to Lord Howard of Effingham and Northampton during one of Howard's visits to the Tower with Robert Cecil. Later, after Essex's execution, the countess of Northampton, on her deathbed, begged for the queen to come to her that she might make a confession before she died. Elizabeth hurried to the countess, one of her closest friends. The countess then told the queen about the ring which she now possessed and of how she had been told to hide it. She begged Elizabeth to forgive her. With a wild scream, Elizabeth grabbed the countess by the shoulders and lifted her off the bed, shaking her and yelling, "I can never forgive you!" The countess fell back on her pillow, dead.

Had Essex tried to reach Elizabeth, and it is possible that he did, his effort would have been easily thwarted by Robert Cecil, who was well situated to intercept any communication.

Cecil was also in a position to convince Elizabeth that Essex had aimed at deposing her and ultimately at taking her life. Both Essex and Southampton had strenuously denied this at their "trial" and had earnestly claimed that their only purpose had been to oust Cecil and his cohorts, who had made repeated attempts to kill them. Nevertheless, Cecil's version prevailed. It prevailed at the trial, it prevailed with Elizabeth, and it has prevailed in the annals of history.

Just before the "Essex Rebellion," the play *Richard II* was performed at the Globe Theatre. An official inquiry followed the arrest of the manager of the company and some of the actors, but the matter was soon dropped and the prisoners released. It was never revealed who had authorized and paid for the performance, but it was hinted that Essex's followers were guilty. Had this been true, the matter surely would have been pursued. It seems clear that the sponsor had to be Cecil himself, for only then would the "inquiry," which was directed by Cecil, have led to naught.

Cecil was quite correct in his estimate of the effect the performance of this play would have on the queen at this particular time. She resented and feared the depiction of an anointed Sovereign's deposition and murder. A good six months after the revolt, on August 4, 1601, Elizabeth remarked during a conference with William Lombarde, Master of the Rolls, "I am Richard The Second, know ye not that"?[1]

The public performances of *Richard II* and Robert Cecil's

clever persuasions had convinced Elizabeth that her situation was precarious and that Essex, a long-time favorite of the general populace, had been the instigator of a wide-spread uprising. The general public was not so easily fooled however. Though Cecil had tried to show that Ralegh was responsible for bringing Essex to "justice," public opinion came firmly down on Cecil himself, and the quips of the ballad-mongers that:

> Little Cecil trips up and down
> He rules both Court and Crown

came very near the truth.[2]

Elizabeth had spent a lifetime exposed to dangers of one sort or another, but now she seemed helpless in the hands of a man who was a master of devious and unscrupulous plotting. Later, in 1605, he would use the same tactics on James I, devising the Guy Fawkes Gunpowder Plot, recently shown to be Cecil's own scheme, to gain the King's confidence and dependency.[3] With Elizabeth, Cecil was in a prime position to manipulate her by playing not only on fears for her own safety but on her anxiety for her son, imprisoned in the Tower and condemned to death. Since William Cecil, Lord Burghley, had succeeded in getting Elizabeth to sign the execution order for Mary, Queen of Scots, she must have worried that his son Robert might manage to get her signature on an order for Southampton's execution.

While Elizabeth lived under considerable stress from concern for her own and her son's safety, as well as the supposed defection of her son and her subjects, she also worried about the intrigues over the succession. Though Cecil was discreet about mentioning the matter in the queen's presence, he was secretly active in making arrangements for James' accession. Neville Williams quotes Cecil as saying, "I am resolved in my mind . . . whom no device nor humor shall make a changeling." 'Make' had the connotation in the sixteenth century of "making" a king. Then Williams continues with the statement that "He (Cecil) was to stage-manage the transition with such adroit circumspection that when the time came there would not be a split second's hesitation in the customary, 'The Queen is dead, long live the King.'"[4]

Cecil may have been making an intentionally oblique allusion to Southampton, the little "changeling child" of *A Midsummer Night' s Dream* . Unfortunately, Neville Williams does not give the source of the incomplete quotation, but there is no question that Lord Burghley, his son Robert, and all members of the Privy Council knew of Elizabeth's children, for the second countess of Southampton had begged Thomas Dymoke many years earlier to have her case heard by the queen and the Privy Council. Now, in his letters Cecil was determined to win the complete confidence of James and warn him of others who had tried soliciting the King's aid, namely, Essex and Southampton, the queen's son.

Since Cecil's plans could succeed only if he kept them utterly secret, he arranged for his correspondence with James to be in cipher. He was determined, too, that "George Nicholson, the English ambassador to Scotland, was on no account to be privy to the negotiations, and James's idea of appointing a resident agent in London had to be discreetly quashed."[5] James had earlier sent two envoys, the earl of Mar and Edward Bruce, to London. Though his original intent was for them to assist Essex, he had received word of the failure of the revolt before they left. He revised the instructions and sent the agents to see "Whether a general rising was still possible and to make it their business to 'dally with the present guiders of the Court' walking warily 'betwixt these two precipices of the queen and the people, who now appear to be in so contrary terms.' "

James also required them to extract from Elizabeth a statement that he had no share in Essex's revolt and they were to be firm with Cecil, who was to be told he could expect no future favors unless he acted favorably towards the King at once.[6]

The queen received James's envoys on March 22 with no cordiality. Following their visit she wrote a letter to James in which she warned him, "Let not shades deceive you, which may take away best substance from you, when they can turn but to dust and smoke."[7]

The earl of Mar and Edward Bruce remained for a while in London. At the end of April 1601 Cecil met with them in secret at the Duchy of Lancaster office in the Savoy. They devised a numbered code to identify various important people: Northumberland was 0, Ralegh was 3, Cecil was 10, the queen 24, and James 30. Neville Williams notes that the numerical progression was "itself a neat piece of psychology."[8] The only other Scot in on the secret was James's secretary, David Foulis, and the only Englishman besides Cecil was Lord Henry Howard. Soon after this Cecil began a regular correspondence with James. Like his father before him, he routinely larded his speeches with maxims and pious phrases. In his letters to James he made a particular point of using classical and Biblical quotations, knowing that they would appeal to the King. He was anxious to win the King's confidence but had to live down past suspicions - "those hard obstructions which other men's practice had bred in your heart."[9]This latter remark was undoubtedly an allusion to the Essex faction, who had sought the King's help in getting rid of Cecil.

Though he had destroyed Essex and his cohorts, and though he had Southampton safely put away in the Tower, there were other groups of courtiers interested in the succession. Northumberland, Ralegh, and Cobham were meeting at Durham House to promote the cause of Protestant King James as Elizabeth's heir, but Cecil must have had his spies planted there because Northumberland's letters to James were intercepted. Cecil also took pains to point out to James that Ralegh had "A pride above the greatest Lucifer that hath lived in our age,"[10] thus eliminating Ralegh from any position of influence with the future King. The culmination of this treatment of Ralegh would be the imprisonment and subsequent beheading of Ralegh on trumped up charges in 1616 - another one of Cecil's victims. Though Cecil died suddenly on April 27, 1612[11] under suspicious circumstances, he had so poisoned James's mind against Ralegh that Cecil was really responsible for Ralegh's eventual execution.

While the Protestant factions were negotiating for James' accession, the English Catholics were trying to make varying arrangements for Elizabeth's successor. While Henry Percy, the Catholic Earl of Northumberland, was writing his advice to James on being tolerant of the loyal Catholics, Lord Howard of Nottingham and Lord Buckhurst were communicating with Catholics in Rome and promoting Isabel, the Infanta of Spain, as Elizabeth's successor. There was such dissension among the

Jesuits and the secular priests for the management of the English Catholics that a proclamation was issued in November of 1602 that all Jesuits must leave England. It is conceivable that Cecil had his hand in that, too. Whether he did or did not, he was still able to assure James that most of the English Catholics, "Do declare their affections absolutely to your title."[11]

While all this was going on, and though Cecil covered his tracks well, Elizabeth was much too shrewd to be taken in. She knew that negotiations were underway and that there were communications with James in Scotland, but for nearly two years everyone quietly waited while Elizabeth steadily lost strength, from both age and worry. Cecil was busy arranging for the transfer of power, and Southampton languished in the Tower, condemned to death, but with his execution indefinitely deferred.

As the year 1602 drew to a close, the queen's godson, Sir John Harrington, reported that Elizabeth was in a state of "great bodily and mental distress." However, she continued to ride and hunt even in bad weather. In January of the new year, 1603, Elizabeth rode from London to Richmond in the company of her cousin, Lord Howard, Earl of Effingham and Northampton. Responding to his queries about the succession, she declared:

> My throne has always been the throne of Kings, and none
> but my next heir of blood and descent ought to succeed
> me.[12]

The above quotation and the rebuke contained in Elizabeth's letter to James both suggest that the queen still planned to leave the crown to her son, Henry Wriothesley, third earl of Southampton. However, a few weeks later the queen's strength failed rapidly in her final decline. Lord Howard, one of the few allowed in her presence at that time, found her much changed and her spirit gone. She complained:

> I am tied with a chain of iron around my neck.[13]

Gently chiding her, Howard asked what had happened to her courage. To this she replied:

> I am tied, I am tied, and the case is altered with me.[14]

Something had happened to the queen to change her whole outlook in a matter of three weeks. The queen's condition grew steadily worse and on March 24 at 3:00a.m. she died in her sleep. A letter written in Latin to Edmund Lambert on the day after her death by someone who may have been one of her doctors states:

> It was after laboring for nearly three weeks under a morbid melancholy, which brought on stupor, not unmixed with some indication of a disordered fancy, that the Queen expired.[15]

The queen's 'morbid melancholy' has never been explained. Perhaps she had been pressured by Cecil, who was in turn being pushed by James. Cecil may have threatened some harm to Southampton, or Elizabeth may have suspected that Cecil planned to poison her to satisfy James impatient urging to see the thing accomplished. The change in her attitude between her determined statement to Lord Howard in late January that her "next heir of blood and descent" should succeed her, and her forlorn cry a few weeks later that "the case was altered," indicates a crisis of some sort.

Whatever that crisis was, it must have been triggered by Cecil, but careful as he was, he left no solid evidence. It would be helpful if the letter in Latin to Edmund Lambert had elaborated on the "indications of the Queen's disordered fancy." She may have tried to convince anyone within hearing that "Prince Hal" was waiting in the Tower for his crown. Cecil, who remained close by as Elizabeth sank to her end, would have been quick to assure those who had heard the queen that she was deranged.

Cecil allowed no reports of the queen's condition to be issued in her last days. It was a game of timing, and he wanted to keep his opponents quiet until he had assured the succession for James. When the queen died on Thursday, Cecil's courier, Sir Robert Carey, the queen's cousin, left immediately to ride north, carrying the news to James. Carey reached Holyrood House Saturday night and knelt before James to greet him as the new King of England.

Cecil, meanwhile, insisted that no one else was to leave Richmond. At 7:00a.m., Cecil and all the councilors rode together to Whitehall to draft a formal Proclamation of Accession. Cecil authoritatively reported to all that the queen's last words had been pronounced on that very day:

> I will that a King succeed me, and who should that be but my nearest kinsman, the King of Scots?[16]

Later a conflicting statement was made:

> But Robert Carey declared that the Queen had been unable to speak at all on the day before she died.[17]

Obviously Cecil was fabricating, but it really did not matter for he had everything and everybody under his control. Those who disagreed with him were too afraid of him to voice any opposition. Significantly, the lowly Secretary Cecil, not some great Lord of the Council, read the formal Proclamation on the steps of Whitehall at ten o'clock on the morning of March 24, 1603. James VI of Scotland was now James I of England.

Before leaving Edinburgh on April 5, James gave the order to release Southampton from the Tower:

> By April 10th Southampton was released and on April 16th James granted him a special pardon with restitution to him and his heirs of his title, lands, and property of all kinds.[18]

Oxford, though deeply grieved by the queen's death, was also comforted by the release of Southampton and was ultimately resigned to James as the new King of England.

Oxford could do no more for Southampton, and Cecil was at last victorious. A short eight years later, however, Cecil died and has been virtually forgotten, while Oxford lives on with his star in the ascendant. Though the Cecils, father and son, did their utmost to emblazon their names as the greatest of English statesmen and endeavored to expunge Oxford from the records, the truth is finally rising to the surface.

In 1603 and 1604, however, Oxford , worn out by illness, anxiety, and frustration, knew that he had not long to live. His last sonnets express resignation and acceptance, though a note of defiance creeps in, too. He knew that his poems, imperishable memorials to his Royal son, would outlive the tyrant Cecils and their "tombs of brass." Oxford had learned that worldly power, material goods, and the flesh itself, were of no importance; it was the spirit, the mind, and what a man's imagination "could body forth".

In Sonnet 107 Oxford tells of his thankfulness for Southampton's release from his "Confin'd doom," his dismay at the death of the queen, and the accession of James:

> Not mine own fears, nor the prophetic soul
> Of the wide world, dreaming on things to come,
> Can yet the lease of my true love control,
> Suppos'd as forfeit to a confin'd doom.
> The mortal moon hath her eclipse endur'd,
> And the sad augurs mock their own presage;
> Uncertainties now crown themselves assur'd,
> And peace proclaims olives of endless age.
> Now with the drops of this most balmy time
> My love looks fresh, and Death to me subscribes,
> Since, spite of him, I'll live in this poor rhyme
> While he insults o'er dull and speechless tribes;
> > And thou in this shalt find thy monument
> > When tyrants' crests and tombs of brass are spent.

Though everyone, including Oxford, had supposed that Southampton (Oxford's "true love," Vere's son) would be entombed in the Tower forever, Oxford's own fears and the world's expectations were unfounded. "The Mortal Moon" (Elizabeth) has endured the final "eclipse" of death.

In lines six through eight, he observes that those who had thought they knew who the King would be were unfortunately wrong. James, who (1) seemed very uncertain as heir to the Throne when Elizabeth wrote to him and warned him not to expect to turn shadows into substance, and (2) who was always known to be timid and afraid of assassination, was an uncertain person, and yet he was now assured of the Crown by Cecil.

"Olives" may be taken two ways: (1) James was known to desire peace (olives represent peace), and (2) "O" (Oxford) lives for an endless age in his poems and plays.

"My love" (my son) looks fresh and well in spite of his imprisonment and Death "subscribes" to Oxford (Oxford has defeated death) because he will live on "in this poor rhyme," but death will overcome those who are dull and speechless (those who may have talked much but with little "matter" (like the Cecils). In the final couplet he assures Southampton that his monument (this sonnet) will outlive the tyrant Cecil's crests and elaborate brass tombs.

Oxford, in failing health, wrote several sonnets that speak of his imminent death. Some are addressed to Southampton, some are his personal ruminations. Perhaps the most perfect of these that combines his own feelings and is also a farewell to his son is Sonnet 73, shown in quatrains:

> That time of year thou mayst in me behold
> When yellow leaves, or none, or few do hang
> Upon those boughs which shake against the cold,
> Bare ruin'd choirs where late the sweet birds sang.
>
> In me thou see'st the twilight of such day
> As after sunset fadeth in the West,
> Which by-and-by black night doth take away,
> Death's second self, that seals up all in rest.
>
> In me thou see'st the glowing of such fire

That on the ashes of his youth doth lie,
As the deathbed whereon it must expire.
Consum'd with that which it was nourish'd by.

This thou perceiv'st, which makes thy love more strong,
To love that well which thou must leave ere long.

The first quatrain of this sonnet uses the imagery of winter (which, in French, is "hiver," a perfect homonym for E. Vere). The second quatrain encompasses a day (Apollo, the sun god, was Oxford's representation at the jousting tournament in 1572). Emphasis is also put on the sun setting in the West (with this latter word capitalized to represent the "Little Western Flower"). The third quatrain depicts one hour's lapse of time. This structure of quickening time from the first to the third quatrain imitates the sensation of the passage of time speeding up as one ages.

The final couplet, if the reader is aware of the whole story behind the name "Shake-speare," is almost unbearably poignant. This sonnet, which is probably the last that he wrote, ends with his unmistakable double signature, "leave ere." This aurally repeats the French translation of his image of "winter," or "L'hiver" of the first quatrain with its homonym E. Vere, and also offers another version of his signature to guarantee it not be missed.

On June 24, 1604 the Earl of Oxford died at Hackney and two things quickly followed. First, the earl of Southampton was again sent to the Tower.

The first year of James's reign had brought Southampton many honors and a number of official assignments that had made him wealthy and influential. Southampton seemed a favorite of both James and Queen Anne.

Akrigg writes:

Suddenly the even happy flow of Southampton's career came to a halt. Late on the evening of June 24th he was arrested, along with Lord Danvers (his old friend, Henry, brother of Charles who was executed after the "Essex Rebellion"), Sir Henry Neville (who had also gone to the Tower after the "rebellion," Sir Maurice Berkeley (a fellow member of Queen Anne's council) and Sir William Lee. Southampton's papers were seized and scrutinized. He himself was interrogated. According to the French Ambassador, King James had gone into a complete panic and could not sleep that night even though he had a guard of his Scots posted around his quarters. Presumably to protect his heir he sent orders to Prince Henry that he must not stir out of his chamber.

Although wild rumors swept through the Court, no facts were ever revealed about the incident. Southampton was quickly found innocent of whatever charges had been brought against him. According to the Venetian and French Ambassadors, he was released on June 25th, the day after his arrest. No documents that relate to this episode survive in either the Public Record Office or in that other great repository of state papers of the period, the Cecil Papers at Hatfield.[22]

Professor Akrigg in a footnote observes:

Sir Anthony Weldon in his scandal mongering Court and Character of King James, (London 1650) P. 41, says that Cecil, to prevent Southampton becoming the royal favorite, played on the King's jealousy. In referring thus to Cecil, Weldon must be mistaken.[23]

Mistaken, yes, but only in the particular emotion that Cecil used to stir the king. He was not playing on the king's jealousy but his fear. Southampton seems to have been safe as long as Oxford was alive. Oxford's pledged fealty to James as king would have precluded any attempt on his part to promote Southampton's rights. The moment Oxford died, however, Cecil must have acted quickly to alert James that Southampton was free to seize his (Southampton's) throne. There is no record that Southampton had made any plans, and it seems doubtful that he was in a position to make a move. Also, the quick dismissal of charges and his prompt release after the search and interrogation seem to indicate that there was no formalized plot.

Southampton was restored to favor, and, according to Professor Akrigg, to compensate Southampton for his unpleasant experience, the king granted him the manor of Romsey in Hampshire, the manor of Compton Magna in Somerset, the manor of Dunmow in Essex, and the grange of Basilden in Gloucester. This largesse seems more likely to be an indication that Southampton signed away all claims to the Throne to gain his release, and that James was, in effect, paying Southampton for his crown.

The other occurrence following Oxford's death was James's tacit tribute to "Great Oxford," as he called him, with the presentation of eight Shakespearean dramas at Court. Later, in 1612 when Oxford's widow, the countess of Oxford died, James presented fourteen of the earl's plays at Court.[24]

This was all the official recognition given England's greatest genius at his death. Even his burial is a mystery, for it is uncertain whether the earl of Oxford is buried in an unmarked grave at Hackney or in an unmarked tomb at Westminster Abbey. Though his widow expressed a desire in her will to be buried beside her late husband at Hackney, there is a reliable report in Louis Golding's book about his ancestor, Arthur Golding (Oxford's uncle), that Oxford was interred at Westminster.

This could mean that Edward de Vere, the seventeenth earl of Oxford, was moved and reburied at some time after his wife died in 1612. It is possible, but may never be proved, that Oxford was reburied after the First Folio was published, and it is also possible that his manuscripts were then buried with him.

In *The Phoenix and The Turtle*, Oxford wrote his Threnos, or lament, for the Royal trio, Beauty, Truth and Rarity:

> Threnos
> Beauty, Truth and Rarity,
> Grace in all simplicity,
> Here enclos'd, in cinders lie.
>
> Truth may seem, but cannot be,
> Beauty brag, but tis not she,
> Truth and Beauty buried be.
>
> To this urn let those repair,
> That are either True or Fair,
> For these dead birds, sigh a prayer.

10 ✤ DREAMING ON THINGS TO COME

SOUTHAMPTON RECEIVED MANY HONORS from King James on his release from the Tower in 1603. Not only was he reinstated as earl of Southampton, but James rescued him from virtual bankruptcy by awarding him the "farm of sweet wines," the same that had supported the earl of Essex for so long during Elizabeth's reign. It was Elizabeth's refusal (influenced by Robert Cecil?) to renew this farm that brought on the crisis leading up to the "Essex Rebellion." According to Professor Akrigg, James regarded Essex as his "martyr" and seemed to be doing his utmost to make amends not only to Southampton but to others who had supported Essex. Among these, Lord Mountjoy, whose brother, Sir Christopher Blount, step-father of Essex, was beheaded after "the rebellion" was made earl of Devonshire. Sir Henry Danvers, whose brother, Sir Charles Danvers, was also beheaded, was created Baron Danvers of Dauntsy.

Though Southampton's farm of sweet wines brought him £8,500 per annum, he was obliged to pay the crown £6000 per annum, as well as bear the expenses of collecting the fees. However, this left him with about £2000 for his own use, which allowed him to live quite well.

James also appointed Southampton Captain of the Isle of Wight. Though the island had always been considered vulnerable to incursions by pirates and England's enemies, Southampton regarded himself as a soldier and welcomed the responsibilities of his Captaincy. He made Carisbrooke Castle his residence on the Isle and superintended the island's defenses. Professor Akrigg notes that Southampton used his own money to repair "the lesser castles at Sandown and Yarmouth." Akrigg then adds the observation that:

> Like the benevolent monarch of a little kingdom, he exercised a calm Saturnian reign, later to be looked back upon with nostalgia by the Island gentry. Sir John Oglander would recall how every Tuesday and Thursday, when the Earl was at his bowling on St. George's Down, thirty to forty knights and gentlemen would join him, eating together and playing bowls and cards.[1]

Though Southampton obviously enjoyed life in his "little island kingdom," other responsibilities drew him back to the larger island that should have been his kingdom. His growing family and his manors at Tichfield and Beaulieu needed attention, and in London obligations to the king required his regular attendance at Court.

Though James was generous to him and seemed to favor him, Southampton never became one of his special intimates. Since the latter was a doubtful honor, he fared better as a friend of Queen Anne. When the

> Queen was provided with a court establishment of her own, with various Lords assigned duties, Southampton was

named "Master of the Queen's game with direction over all Her Majesty's forests and chases."[2]

One encounter with his old enemy Lord Grey at Windsor in the Queen's presence had rather serious consequences. In chatting with Southampton the Queen spoke with wonder that, "so many great men did so little for themselves" (referring to the Essex Rebellion). The Earl's response was that they had no choice but to yield, since their sovereign had sided with their enemies. He added that without Queen Elizabeth's support none of the private enemies of Essex and himself would have dared to oppose them.[3]

Standing nearby and overhearing this exchange, Lord Grey asserted that he and his friends could have done much more than the Essex faction. A quarrel broke out and Queen Anne sent both parties to their lodgings and put them under guard. Though the Privy Council was prepared to send both Southampton and Lord Grey to the Tower the following day, King James interceded and allowed them to go free.

A short two weeks later, Grey was arrested for involvement in the Bye Plot. At Grey's trial on December 7, Southampton sat on the jury, just as Lord Grey had been a juror at Essex's and Southampton's trial four years earlier. One can only imagine what Southampton must have felt when this man who had tried several times to kill him and who had fomented so much trouble for him and his cousin Essex was condemned to death. Grey, his sentence commuted at the last moment to life in prison (due to Cecil's intervention?), spent the last ten years of his life in the Tower, dying without a son to continue his ancient line.[4]

Southampton's family, on the other hand, was thriving. In

1603 a second daughter was born and named for Queen Anne. In March of 1605 a son, James, heir to the Southampton title, was born and named for the king, who stood as godfather at the christening. Also serving as godfather was Robert Cecil, the newly made Viscount Cranbourne. Three years later a second son, Thomas, was born, giving added assurance that the Southampton title would be continued.

As his family grew, Southampton seemed to spend more time living a quiet life at Beaulieu in Hampshire. According to Professor Akrigg, the King visited Southampton at Beaulieu in 1609, 1611, 1613, 1618, and 1623. Akrigg also reports the earl's visit to "Althorp, the great Northamptonshire home of Lord Spencer. The date is uncertain, but probably some time after the marriage of Southampton's eldest daughter, Penelope, to the Spencer heir."[5] From this marriage of Lady Penelope Wriothesley to the Spencer heir early in the seventeenth century, the Tudor-Vere lineage descends in a direct line to the late Diana Spencer Windsor, Princess of Wales and to her sons, Prince William and Prince Henry. This means that the youngest Windsors combine in their bloodlines the Normans, the Plantagenets, the Tudors, and the Saxe-Coburg-Windsors.

Another important observation by Akrigg is that Southampton:

> cut a figure at Court, but he was never appointed to any position of real political power. A Knight of the Garter in 1603, he had to wait until April 1619 for the seat on the Privy Council that he eagerly desired. . .
>
> It was probably on Cecil's advice that King James established his policy of giving Southampton honours and

money but not political power . . . it was not disloyalty to Southampton but simple fulfilment of his duty to the King . . . In any event, with the passing of Cecil a new era began for Southampton.[6]

The passing of Cecil in 1612 would indeed have made a change in Southampton's life. The man who had successfully plotted to take his Crown from him had used every stratagem possible to maintain control of James, thereby eliminating any chance that Southampton might gain power. Had Southampton been given a role in the government, he might have gained enough strength, popular as he was, to have brought Cecil to trial before the Council to be judged for treason against the state and his sovereign. He must have often wished for the opportunity to sit in judgment of Cecil as he had earlier in the trial of Lord Grey. However, Cecil endured another sort of trial in his long, painful illness before he died, which is now thought to have been cancer of the stomach.

After Cecil's death in 1612, Southampton did enter into the power struggles at Court but without success. James's personal favorites controlled him from that time on. First there was the Scot Robert Carr, created Viscount Rochester by James, who gained power, and then George Villiers charmed James, was made Marquess of Buckingham, and took complete control of James.

At first, Southampton was on friendly terms with Buckingham, who was responsible for the earl's appointment to the Privy Council. Soon, however, Buckingham's arrogance and advancement of his relatives, as well as his urging of a marriage between Prince Charles and the Spanish Infanta, caused a rift between them.[7]

In the Parliament of 1621 Southampton was the leader of a faction opposing the "Kings Party," which was led by Buckingham.

> ...in both Houses the King had a strong Party, especially in the House of Lords: All the Courtiers, and most of the Bishops, steer'd by his Compass, and the Prince's Presence (who was a constant member) did cast an Awe among many of them, yet there were some gallant spirits that aimed at the publick Liberty, more than their own Interest...among which the Principal were, Henry Earl of Oxford, Henry Earl of Southampton, Robert Earl of Essex, Robert Earl of Warwick, the Lord Say, the Lord Spencer, and divers others that supported the old English Honour, and would not let it fall to the ground.[8]

Southampton's championing of the people's interests seems to indicate that he would have been a benign ruler, genuinely concerned with the welfare of his subjects, had he inherited the throne. Had the self-serving and hedonistic Stuarts remained in Scotland, there might have been no civil war, no Commonwealth, and no Restoration, with all the accompanying upheaval and loss of life. It is interesting that the list of lords who sided with Southampton in the Parliamentary faction included the eighteenth earl of Oxford and the third earl of Essex, brave sons of men who in their own time had been known for their honesty and idealism.

Southampton's minority group opposing Buckingham and the King's Party in the House of Lords was working closely with a majority group in the Commons led by Sir Edwin Sandys. The king, in a fury at such opposition, quickly adjourned Parliament and ordered that the Privy Council commit Southampton to the custody of the Dean of Westminster, and the leader of the Commons faction, Sir Edwin Sandys, was arrested and turned over to the Sheriffs of London.[9]

Examined by a special commission, Southampton was asked if "his own conscience did not accuse him of unfaithfulness to the King in the Latter parte of the parliament." He denied that he had "ever any desseine or plott." He did, however, admit that unkindness might exist between him and persons near to the king, but denied that he had said that there would "never be a gud reformacon whyle one [Buckingham] did so wholy governe the King."[10]

He was next accused of having said he disliked attending Privy Council meetings because there were "soe many boyes and base fellowes there." This was also denied, but it is quite likely that he had been too outspoken about the dissolute and debauched behavior of the monarch and his favorites. Interestingly, shortly afterwards Henry, earl of Oxford and Southampton's half-brother, was arrested, "apparently for too bold speech in behalf of the earl of Southampton." A portrait of the two Henry's shown together dressed in battle armor and on horseback, indicates that they were devoted to each other in spite of a twenty-year difference in age. Evidently the younger Henry was quick of tongue and staunch in support of his older brother.

At this time, however, Southampton evidently solved his own problems by making friends with his warder, John Williams, Dean of Westminster, who was one of Buckingham's proteges. Akrigg reports that "a brisk, knowledgeable little Welshman, Williams was in this same month of July 1621 appointed Lord Keeper of the Great Seal, replacing the disgraced Bacon."[11]

Though Bacon had been tried for bribery and sent to the Tower, he was no more guilty than his predecessors but was following the customary habit of the office. It looks as though his removal was aimed at providing one of Buckingham's men with a lucrative job. Nevertheless, Williams and Southampton shared a taste for books and learning and, though Williams was of a later generation, both men had attended St. John's College at Cambridge. Akrigg adds a footnote to this that several years later Williams would contribute two-thirds of the cost of the new library built at St. John's in consequence of Southampton's gift of the Crashaw books and manuscripts.[12]

The two men soon became such good friends that Williams opened the way to a pardon for Southampton. First, he arranged for Buckingham to talk with the earl at the Deanery, and then, two days later Buckingham took Southampton to Theobalds for a conference with the King. On their return to London Williams escorted the earl to Southampton House in Holburn and left him there with instructions that he return to Tichfield and remain there under the watch of Sir William Parkhurst. At the end of August he was given complete freedom.[13]

Though ostensibly free, Southampton was warned not to attend Parliament when it reconvened in November. It was just as well that he remained in Tichfield at that time. James, in a flaming rage, tore out pages of the journal of the House of Commons and summarily dissolved Parliament.[14]

Southampton had other interests at this time and scarcely had time to attend Parliamentary session. In April of 1619, Southampton's friend Sir Edwin Sandys had taken over as Treasurer of the Virginia Company. When his election came up for renewal, King James would not allow Sandys to be re-elected.

Not only was Sandys the leader of the anti-King's Party faction in the Commons, but James resented the profits earned by the colonists raising that noxious weed tobacco. James had approved Southampton's election to the office of Treasurer—or Governor—of the Virginia Company and wrote him "to take speedy order that our people there use all possible diligence in breeding silkewormes."[15] Orders from England had little effect on the activities and events in Virginia. On Good Friday in 1622 more than 350 colonists were killed in an Indian massacre. The following year in January the colony was decimated by the plague.[16]

Meanwhile in England the Virginia Company was almost bankrupt, and different factions were scrambling for control of the company. Eventually King James appointed a commission to report on the company's affairs. Southampton was told to postpone elections for that year, and soon the government called in the Virginia Company's charter and determined to transfer control to the Privy Council. When the company refused to surrender the charter, the Crown began proceedings in the Court of the King's Bench, and in May, 1624 the Court ruled, not surprisingly, in favor of the Crown. The Virginia Company then became a Crown Colony.[17]

Southampton somehow during these final months of the company managed to retain the good opinion of both King James and the shareholders. "On November 19th, 1623, the dying company granted him twenty shares of land in the colony because he 'hath ever since the eight and twentieth day of June Anno 1620 intill this present performed the place of Treasuror of this company with singular wisdom providence and care and much Noble paynes and Industrie and with unquestionable integritie.'"[18]

Southampton had made other investments in explorations. He had become a shareholder in the East India Company in 1609 and invested more in 1620 and 1621. Large tracts of land, rivers, and islands in the New World still bear Southampton's title or some variation of it.

In 1623 Southampton was living quietly at Tichfield with his family and enjoying his life in retirement. On the day before Christmas in 1623 he wrote a letter to an old friend, Sir Thomas Roe:

> . . . in this life I have fownd so much quiett & content that I thinke I should hardly ever brooke any other, sure I am I envy none, & shall unwillingly leave this if any occation shall draw mee from it.[19]

All too soon, though, he would be asked to help his country once more. Early in June of 1624 he was called to serve in the Netherlands against Spain and the Austrian Hapsburgs. The latter had encroached on James's daughter and son-in-law's lands in Bohemia. Frederick and Elizabeth barely escaped from Bohemia with their lives. Jame's son Prince Charles had been negotiating a marriage with the Spanish Infanta and had even made a trip to Spain with Buckingham to settle the marriage contract, in hopes that by doing so they could persuade Spain to intercede with the Austrians. These negotiations proved useless, and they now declared war against both Spain and Austria.

Charles and Buckingham, who was now elevated to a duke, were in charge of war operations. Their first step was to make a treaty with the Dutch, who were already at war with Spain.

Envoys from The Hague negotiated an agreement that required the English to raise four regiments with a total of six thousand men. The regiments would not serve as an English army but would serve under a Dutch command. Southampton was offered a command but was reluctant to accept it and suggested that it be given to his nineteen-year-old son, Lord Wriothesley. "Even by 17th-century standards, however, a boy of nineteen was hardly old enough to command fifteen hundred men in the field, even though he may perhaps have already seen some military service under Horace Vere."[20] It is interesting to note how many of Edward de Vere's sons and grandsons were trained under either Horace or Francis Vere.

Southampton was pressed by Prince Charles to take the command himself. According to Akrigg, the Prince and Buckingham counted on the drawing power of Southampton in recruiting the six thousand volunteers.

Southampton finally agreed to serve. "Early in June 1624, the Dutch envoys signed the letters patent appointing their colonels:

Henry Wriothesley, Earl of Southampton
Henry Vere, Earl of Oxford
Robert Devereux, Earl of Essex
Robert Bertie, Lord Willoughby"[21]

Of these four officers, two were Edward de Vere's sons and one, Bertie, was his nephew.

". . . a troublesome little problem of precedence arose between Southampton and Oxford, Fortunately, in an age when such an issue could provoke a major quarrel, the two earls conducted themselves moderately."[22]

The king finally settled the matter by ruling that "the earl of Oxford shall have precedency in all civil and courtly passages and actions, and the earl of Southampton in all martial and military passages."[23]

In August Southampton sailed for Holland, and at the end of August the English colonels were escorted by the English ambassador to the Assembly of the States General where they swore their oaths of fealty.[24]

Three months later, in November, Southampton's regiment, then in winter quarters at Roosendaal, was stricken with a severe fever. On November 5, young Lord Wriothesley, who had accompanied his father to war, died of the fever. His father was ill, too, but seemed to recover. He began the long trip home with the body of his son but he died on the way. Akrigg quotes a report by Arthur Wilson, who wrote an account of the event:

> . . . the drooping father having overcome the fever, departed from Rosendale with the intention to bring his Son's body into England, but at Berghen-op-Zoom he died of a lethargy in the View and Presence of the Relator, and were both in one small Bark brought to Southampton.[25]

Southampton's widow was inconsolable in her grief, and many others seem to have felt the loss almost as much. Southampton may have been wild and reckless in his youth, but he had endeared himself to all in his mature years. One wonders whether history would have been kinder to the English people in the seventeenth century had they been ruled by a kind and careful King Henry IX.

When Henry died, his second son, Thomas, became the fourth earl of Southampton.

He became Lord Treasurer of England under Charles II, and was noted for his wisdom, humanity, and integrity. He left no male heir and so his earldom ended with him. Three of his daughters survived into married life. By his first wife, Rachel de Ruvigny, he was father of Elizabeth, from whom have descended the Dukes of Portland, and Rachel, from whom have descended the Dukes of Bedford. By his second wife, Elizabeth Leigh, he fathered another daughter Elizabeth, from whom are descended the Dukes of Buccleuch and the Lords Montagu of Beaulieu.[26]

As we have already noted, the inheritance through Thomas' sister Penelope has carried the family line down to the young Royal heirs of the House of Windsor. This means that they have a heritage that combines the great British Royal families with the most extraordinary, myriad-minded genius of the English-speaking world, "Shake-speare," also known as Edward de Vere, the seventeenth earl of Oxford.

"Good night, sweet prince,
And flights of angels sing thee to thy rest!"

APPENDIX A ⁓ The Southampton Tower Portrait

The third earl of Southampton's 'Tower Portrait' was painted soon after his release from the Tower. It seems curious that he would wish to dwell on his dreary days of captivity as well as the probable fear he endured, wondering if he might still be sent to the block. If the Queen had allowed her special favorite, the earl of Essex, to be executed, Southampton must have wondered when his turn might come. Though sentenced to death originally, his sentence had been commuted to life imprisonment. Yet, there was really no guarantee that the lesser sentence would stand indefinitely. As long as he remained in the Tower, he was in jeopardy. Perhaps then, Southampton's purpose in having this experience preserved in a portrait after his release may be revealed in the *impresa*, or symbols, in the portrait itself.

The most obvious symbol in this remarkable painting is the small inset in the upper right corner, which in the sixteenth century was commonly used to identify and characterize the sitter. For instance, Southampton's inset features the Tower of London where he spent so many weary months, but that's not all. There is more symbolism in the foreground of this miniature picture, which shows the Thames River and some swans swimming in rather rough water.

By the rules of *impresa* the swans and the river in the foreground must have a message, too. British citizens today still respect the status of these swans as Royal Swans. No one may touch them but the Royal Swan Keepers. In the sixteenth century tampering with Royal Swans called for the death penalty. The swans in this instance are swimming with some difficulty in very turbulent waters. This could therefore translate to, "Royalty swimming in turbulent waters" and carrying that over to the sitter being portrayed, he is seen as "Royalty in serious trouble". Thus, if the Tower prisoner was Royal, it could have been the reason why those who condemned him and sent him to the Tower with the other members of the so-called Essex Rebellion did not dare to execute the earl of Southampton, if he was a Royal heir.

In 1547, Henry VIII executed the earl of Surrey for merely quartering his Royal York Arms in a newly-built chapel in the remoteness of northern England. Surrey, though descended from the Royal York Kings, was not a possible heir to the throne. He was noble, but not Royal, yet Henry VIII was furious when Surrey used the York arms even as a quarter section of his crest. Thus, using a Royal symbol in a portrait could cause serious trouble if it were not a valid claim.

Other *impresa* in the portrait are significant, too. A book on the table beside Southampton has a green ribbon page-marker that defies gravity to create the letter E (viz: Σ). This could represent Southampton's wife, Elizabeth, or the queen, or both. Since green was one of the queen's special colors, it does seem this was meant to refer to Queen Elizabeth.

The portrait shows Southampton wearing a glove on his right hand, with his forefinger pointing to the floor which may indicate he was a Mason. His bare left hand has long, slim fingers, just like Queen Elizabeth's.

A black and white cat sits by the window, staring at the viewer with a penetrating glare. There is an old story in a book, *Of London*, written by Thomas Pennant in 1790, that it was Southampton's cat that found its way to his owner and came down the chimney to stay with him during his captivity. The cat could also suggest the old saying that cats have nine lives. Leslie Hotson, in *Mr. W.H.* claims, "The cat is merely an iconographical symbol saying, 'Give me back my freedom'." In Southampton's case the latter view seems appropriate since he languished in the Tower for many months condemned to life in prison. Though he had escaped the fate of the other rebels, he may have felt he had used several 'cat lives'. One of these was just prior to the 'rebellion', when Robert Cecil's troops had shot at him and he escaped with only a bullet-hole in his hat. He used up another 'cat life' by surviving the actual gunfire at Essex House during the rebellion, and another when he escaped death once more with his sentence commuted to imprisonment. Thus the cat in the picture may represent Southampton's many escapes from certain death.

It seems surprising no one has ever explained why Southampton, alone, had his death sentence commuted to 'Life in Prison'. Nor has it been explained why King James gave the order to release Southampton before he reached London.

A second issue never addressed is the assignment of Robert Cecil's friend, Sir John Peyton, as Warden of the Tower when the members of the Essex Rebellion were sent to the Tower. Nor has there been any reason given why, immediately after James gave the order to release Southampton, Peyton was removed from the office of Warden. This seems to indicate Robert Cecil wielded far more power than that of a mere secretary to the queen.

The queen was at Richmond with all the members of the Court when she went into her decline and finally into a coma. At 3:00am on Thursday, 24 March, she died in her sleep.

Robert Cecil insisted that no one leave Richmond Palace without written authority, while he and the Councillors present rode to Whitehall for a formal meeting to draft the Accession Proclamation. Northumberland maintained that councilors had no status in acting during an interregnum, and that senior peers should take their places of right. Lord Keeper Egerton saw the force of the argument, but treated it as merely a question of precedence, ruling that Privy Councillors who were not peers should sit at the lower end of the table. Significantly it was Robert Cecil who performed the first reading of the Proclamation at Whitehall Palace, opposite the tiltyard, for he had single-handed(ly) made sure of James's peaceful accession.[1]

Cecil claimed the queen indicated just before she died that James should be king, but he did not mention the queen's inability to speak for several days, or her comatose condition, for more than a week. Nor did he mention he had communicated secretly with James for many months. Cecil's power, however, seemed to be no secret, for ballad mongers had been singing a ditty on street corners for some time before Cecil became a key figure in the accession of James:

Little Cecil trips up and down
He rules both Court and Crown[2]

James did not seem Queen Elizabeth's choice to succeed her. Some months before she went into her final decline, she received a letter from him. In her response, she warned him not to count on inheriting her throne, saying, "Do not of a shadow a substance make". This Platonic reference to the Fable of the Cave was also used by the earl of Oxford in several instances, one of which was in a letter to Lord Burghley.

Thus, we have, firstly, the *impresa* of the portrait indicating Southampton was Royal. Secondly, we have indications Robert Cecil held extraordinary power for a lowly secretary. Then, most importantly, we have a queen who said clearly in her own handwritten letter, she did not intend to put James VI of Scotland on the English throne.

These are the main threads running through *Shakespeare and the Tudor Rose.*

1 *All The Queen's Men*; Neville Williams, p. 261
2 Ibid., p. 241

APPENDIX B ❦ The Darling Buds Of May:
Non Sequitur, Allegory, and Impresa

We sometimes need to remind ourselves that all 'Oxfordians'
were originally 'Stratfordians'. Some people are introduced to
an alternative author for Shakespeare by hearing a lecture or
by reading about the controversy, but for some there is a moment of revelation as we encounter one or more *non sequiturs* in
the 'Shakespeare' biography. Whatever has brought us to the
Oxford theory of authorship, we are eager to know more about
this person's life experiences and character and thus have a
better understanding of the author's works.

Yet, knowing that Edward de Vere, the seventeenth earl of
Oxford, was 'Shakespeare', we find such conflicting reports that
this knowledge may not be exactly what we expect or want to
hear. In spite of this, we should not wear blinders or forget for
a moment that he was a human being. If we are to understand
him and his works, we must accept him as he was, and not expect him to be a miracle of perfection. Part of his genius was
his clear recognition of the human condition; with all the good
and the bad of human nature combined. Those who have shied
away from Oxford's experiences because they seem to diminish his heroic profile have deprived themselves of a much deeper
aesthetic and philosophic experience.

Some Oxfordians, when asked why these works were hidden behind the pseudonym 'William Shakespeare', quickly re-
spond, "It was beneath his dignity as a nobleman to publish
under his own name." That simply does not make sense. Even

the author tells us, in Sonnet 66, that he is "tongue tied by authority". This official silencing is something that needs an explanation, not a platitude.

Primary sources are admittedly important in our research of Oxford, but there's a distinct paucity of information as well as mysterious blanks in his records. To a great extent, his life was centered in the Court of Queen Elizabeth I and yet he traveled abroad on an extended trip to France and Italy, with a side trip to visit Sturmius in Strasbourg. There are hints that his Italian visit included a side trip to Eastern Mediterranean countries, but without records we can only surmise this from scenes in his plays.

There should be records of Oxford's activities at Queen Elizabeth's Court but, though there are records of Court business and entertainments, many records were lost, destroyed, or hidden when Lord Burghley was in charge from 1558 to his death in 1598. There is, however, one alternative source of records left by foreign ambassadors, whose letters to their respective homelands provide us with reports which may be quite biased, but which are also informative. Occasionally, private letters have been preserved for some reason and they can sometimes solve great mysteries of the sixteenth century.

Another fund of information where primary sources have not survived are in the plays that were written as allegory. Though they have a perfectly reasonable surface meaning, there is also an allegorical hidden meaning that reveals many secrets about the author as well as of sixteenth century politics, both domestic and foreign. Recent studies on allegory in Shakespeare's plays, by Mildred Sexton of St. Louis, have been a revelation to Shakespeare researchers. Looking below the surface, we learn much about the author and his views. Taking 'allegory' one step further, we may also find revelations in Shakespeare's Sonnets, in *Venus and Adonis*, *The Rape of Lucrece*, and in *The Phoenix and the Turtle*.

Perhaps the single most controversial mystery about Oxford as Shakespeare is his relationship with Henry Wriothesley, third earl of Southampton, to whom the first publication under the name of William Shakespeare, *Venus and Adonis*, was dedicated. For several centuries, it was supposed that the earl of Southampton had been a generous sponsor for Shakespeare. To prove this fact, and in hope of thus finding more information about the author, Charlotte Stopes thoroughly researched the life of Southampton and, in 1925, published her 'disappointing results' in her *Biography of Henry Wriothesley, Third Earl of Southampton*. She felt she had failed miserably because she could find no evidence of the earl supporting or even contacting, 'Shakespeare'. Her research was not wasted effort though, for she provided a new generation of scholars with some critically important information.

Almost at the beginning of her book, we encounter a footnote on page two, an item that could be of importance:

> It has always been said he (Southampton) was 'the second son', but there is no authority for that. The error must have begun in confusing the second with the first Henry (the 2nd Earl).

Mrs. Stopes, having previously stated in her preface, "From a plain statement of facts ... we may sometimes secure legitimate inferences," she has indeed done this in the quoted footnote above. In this case, she may be emending the statement in her own mind to make sense of her preconceived view of the third earl of Southampton. If, instead of accepting Mrs. Stopes' version, we view the statement in a simpler way, that Henry was indeed the second son, then we have an important bit of information. There is a letter, preserved at the Folger Library written by the second earl of Southampton, from his father-in-law's home in Cowdrey, and sent to his friend, Sir Thomas More of Losely, in which he tells of a son born on October 6, 1573. The letter does not include that son's name.

According to reports given to Mrs. Stopes, there was another son in the Wriothesley family, but the records do not tell what happened to the other child, or what his name was. Therefore, it is possible that there was another son. Let us suppose that this first son was named William for the second earl's good friend and warder, Sir William More of Losely. The second earl of Southampton had spent five months as a prisoner in the Tower of London on a charge of recusancy. Though given his release from the Tower, he had only limited freedom under the guardianship of Sir William at Losely. The earl and his warder soon became close friends. If the first son was named William in honor of this friend and guardian, it solves another mystery. It would explain why the second earl of Southampton added a codicil in his will, "To William my beggar boy," a legacy of £80 to pay for his education until he reached the age of 21.

After a few months at Losely, Wriothesley was allowed to move to his father-in-law Lord Montague's estate at Cowdrey when their son was born, and it was from there that the earl sent his letter to Sir William More announcing the birth of their son.

Not long after this, the Wriothesleys were allowed to return to their home at Beaulieu, but they remained under guard.

This time, their guardian was Thomas Dymoke, a young

man of a prominent family at Queen Elizabeth's court, who had just finished his law studies in London. This Thomas Dymoke served the earl as 'Gentleman of the Bed Chamber'. This is certainly a non sequitur for a well-born young lawyer to serve in this capacity, but it is even more surprising to find that he was also a great-grandson of Sir Edward Dymoke, Queen Elizabeth's ceremonial Champion at her coronation. Furthermore, members of this family had served as the monarch's Champion at coronations as far back as Richard II[1]. This same Thomas Dymoke serving the earl also eventually became Sir Thomas Dymoke. Thus we find, not one, but a cluster of non sequiturs.

Although the Wriothesleys had finally returned to their own home, there was trouble brewing under the Dymoke guardianship. The countess made repeated visits to one of their properties at Dogmersfield. For some reason she was warned by Dymoke to stay away from Dogmersfield, but she continued traveling the few miles to this farm property owned by the Wriothesleys. This, too, seems to be a non sequitur. Why would Dymoke restrict the countess's visits to one of their own properties? One possibility for the countess's repeated trips could be a mother's need to see her real son, William, if he had been removed from the Wriothesley household at Beaulieu and placed in the care of a man named Donsame, the manager of their property at Dogmersfield.

The countess, defying Dymoke's order, was caught once more at Dogmersfield. And Dymoke then confined the her in a cottage on the Beaulieu estate. Why would Dymoke have the right to separate the Wriothesleys and imprison the countess? Once more, we find a cluster of non sequiturs with Dymoke again at the center of the action.

Not long after these incidents, the second earl's health began to trouble him and after some months of illness, he died. Dymocke had drawn up a will for the earl as his health was deteriorating, but at some time the earl found an opportunity to add two codicils to his will. One was the aforementioned legacy for "William, my Beggar Boy", the other was the gift of a ring to his father-in-law "in perfect love and charity". This, too, is a non sequitur since Dymocke had said there was dissention between the two families, extending even to the servants of both families The so-called disruption between the families seems again to be the creation of Dymocke[2].

After the second earl's death, the countess appealed to her powerful cousin, the earl of Leicester, to intercede with the queen and to have some of the benefits for Dymocke removed from the will, for he had written the will to benefit himself and would have received most of the Wriothesly properties. In Mrs. Stopes' book, she quotes a letter written by the widowed countess of Southampton to the earl of Leicester:

> Mr. Dymocke voyde of either wytte, ability or honesty to dischardg the same (i.e. the will) doth so vexe me as in troth my Lord I am not able to expresse. How to better yt I know no menes to her Majestie but by your menes to her to have consideracion of the man, and *gret matters that resteth in his hands unaccomptable but by Her Prerogative*, which I trust by your Lordship's menes to procure for the *good of the child*. (italics added)[3]

Dymocke has been given charge of "great matters" for the queen while ostensibly acting as a servant in the Wriothesly household. Another letter from the countess to Leicester speaks in the same vein about "the child" as opposed to "my child" or "my son":

> Yf possibly yt may be, which truly my Lord can never be (without great hinderance to *the child*) except such travell (i.e. travail) and paynes which may ever be taken *for it* as I know none can or wyll do, but he who is tyed to *the child* both in nature and kinship. That your Lordship shall judge my Lord, my father his meaning or myne, is not to make an *undutyfull motion to her Majestie or her state*.[4]

The countess speaks of "the child", refers to "yt", "great matters" and her duty to the Queen. The countess must have been truly desperate to make such a plea, even though her intermediary, Leicester, was close to the queen.

Ben Jonson speaks of matters in "High Places" in *Batholomew Fair*, written in 1596 but not performed until 1614. Would it have been risky to perform it earlier?

> Act I, scene 6:
> Zeal-of-the-Land-Busy:... Now pig is a meat, and meat that is nourishing, and may be longed for, and so consequently eaten; it may be eaten: very exceeding well eaten. But, in the *Fair*, and as a *Barthol'mew-pig* it cannot be eaten. For the *very* calling it a *Barthol'mew pig* and to eat it so, is a spice of *idolatry*, and you make the Fair no better than *one of the high places*. This I take it is the state of the question. *A High Place*. (Italics added).

The quotation from Jonson echoes Shakespeare. In *Henry IV 2*, act II, scene 4, Doll Tearsheet calls Falstaff "Thou little tidy Bartholmew Boar Pig." The word "Idolatry" is a central feature of Shakespeare's Sonnet 105:

Let not my love be call'd **idolatry**
Nor my beloved as an **Idoll** show
Since all alike my songs and praises be
To one, of one, still such, and **ever** so,
Kinde is my love today and tomorrow **kind**,
Still **constant** in a wondrous excellence,
Therefore my **ver**se to **constancie** confin'de
One thing expressing, leaves out difference.
Faire, Kinde, and True, is all my argument,
Faire Kinde and True, varying to other words.
And in this change is my invention spent,
Three themes in one, which wondrous scope affords.
    Faire, Kinde and True, have often liv'd alone.
    Which three till now, never kept seat in one.

The word 'kind' has several meanings. 'Kind' is German for 'child'. There is also a now obsolete usage meaning ' sprung' or 'begotten'. The Oxford English Dictionary also lists the first meaning of 'Nature' as birth and adds that the native English word for 'birth' is 'kind'. There is also a Middle English or Old English usage in numerous combinations with the sense of 'kingly' or 'royal'. Hamlet speaks with fervor when he observes that Claudius is "a little more than 'kin' and a little less than 'kind'." Does he mean "Less than Royal"?

While Jonson's portrayal of Burghley as 'Zeal-of-the-Land-Busy' is not as deft as the Polonius/Burghley in Hamlet it does seem to be what was intended. Another main character, 'Littlewit', seems to represent Burghley's son-in-law, Oxford. The name could either mean a small man with a sharp wit, or a man with little wisdom. Littlewit's wife, 'Win', pretending to be pregnant, claims she has a craving for roast pig served by 'Ursa' the pig woman at her tent in the middle of the Fair. Ursa, the Bear was the insignia of the goddess, Diana and Diana represents the queen. Ursa seems to be a crude representation of Queen Elizabeth and her small assistant at the roast pig tent is "mooncalf". There was indeed good reason why the play was never performed until 1614 when not only Queen Elizabeth was dead, but Robert Cecil as well.

Ben Jonson also wrote two interesting poems that are relevant. The first is addressed "To His much and worthily esteemed Friend The Author":

> Who takes thy volume to his vertuous hand,
> Must be intended still to understand:
> Who bluntly doth but looke upon the same
> May ask, *What author would conceal his name?**
> Who reads may roave, and call the passage dark,
> Yet may as blind men hit the marke.
>
> (* Italics are in the original)

The second poem is quite astonishing:

The Phoenix Analyzed

> Now, after all, let no man
> Receive it for a fable
> If a bird so amiable,
> Do turn into a **woman**.
> Or (by our **Turtles Augure**)
> That **Nature's Fairest Creature**,
> Prove of his **Mistris Feature**

But a **bare type and Figure**.

Note that '**Alyzed**' sounds like 'Elize'. The Phoenix in line four has become a woman, but the title of the poem has already given a hint aurally that she's "Elize" or Queen Elizabeth. "Turtle's Augure" ties the 'Turtle' to Shakespeare's poem, *The Phoenix and the Turtle*. It also refers to the final couplet of Shakespeare's Sonnet 14: "Or else of thee this I prognosticate | Thy end is Truth's and Beauty's doom and date." In Sonnet 1, the second line shows concern for the demise of 'Beauty's Rose': "That thereby Beauty's Rose might never die."

"Natures Fairest Creature" echoes Sonnet One. 'Nature' was often used to refer to Queen Elizabeth. "Prove of his 'mistris' Feature/But a Bare (Bear-Ursa-Diana-Elizabeth) Type and Figure." Type" means 'image' or 'representation' and 'Figure' is 'likeness' according to the Oxford English Dictionary. Thus Jonson seems to be boldly referring to the queen, Oxford and Southampton.

SONNET 14

Not from the stars do I my judgement pluck
And yet methinks I have astronomy;
But not to tell of good or evil lucke
Of plagues, of dearths of season's quality;
Nor can I fortune to breefe mynnuites tell,
Pointing to each his thunder, raine, and winde,
Or say with Princes if it shall go wel.
By oft predict that I in heaven find
But from **thine eies** my knowledge I derive,
And **constant stars**, in them I read such art
As **Truth and Beautie** shal together thrive

If from thyself to store thou wouldst convert
   Or else of the(e) this I prognosticate
   Thy end is Truthes and Beauties doome and date.[5]

It is important to see at least part of *The Phoenix and the Turtle* in juxtaposition with Sonnet 14 to demonstrate the relationship of the two poems. It shows that the Turtles Augure did indeed prove true, for after the so-called Essex Rebellion (induced by Robert Cecil's attempts to assassinate Southampton) it was indeed their 'doom and date' dynastically.

Here the Antheme doth commence
Love and **Constancy** is dead
Phoenix and the Turtle fled
In a mutual flame from hence.

Hearts remote yet not asunder,
Distance and no space was seene
Twixt this **Turtle** and his **Queene**
But in them it were a wonder

So between them love did shine,
That the **Turtle** saw his right,
Flaming in the **Phoenix** sight,
Either was the others mine

Property was thus appalled
That the selfe was not the same,
Single **Natures** double name,
Neither two nor one was called.
Whereupon it made this **threne**
To the **Phoenix** and the **Dove**

Co-supremes and starres of love,
As *chorus* to their tragique Scene.

Threnos

Beautie, Truthe and Raritie[6]
Grace in all simplicity
Here enclosed in cinders lie

Death is now the *Phoenix Nest*,
And the **Turtles** loyall brest,
To eternitie doth rest.

Truth may seem, but cannot be
Beautie bragge, but tis not she,
Truth and Beautie buried be.

To this urne let those repaire,
That are either **true** or **Faire**,
For these dead birds sigh a prayer.

The penultimate verse of *The Phoenix and the Turtle* is indeed a tragic match for the augury of Sonnet 14. Note the echo of Constancy in "Constant stars" in the same Sonnet as well as in Sonnet 105. Compare the use of "rare" in Sonnet 56, third quatrain, to the first line of the *Threnos*:

Let this sad int'rim like the ocean be
Which parts the shore where **two contracted new**
Come daily to the bankes, that when they see
Return of love, more blest may be the view.
As cal it **winter**, which being ful of care,

Makes somers welcome, **thrice** more wish'd, more **rare**

Note particularly, "Two contracted new" and "somer's welcome" and "Thrice" representing the family of three. "Rare" echoes the "rarity" in the first line of the Threnos in *Phoenix*. "Winter" in French is "hiver" and should be noted as the homonym for E. Vere.

Two short verses that originally preceded the *Phoenix and the Turtle* and are usually omitted from modern publications, appeared in the Grossart Edition as printed below.

The First

The silver vault of heaven, hath but one Eie,
And that's the sunne, the foul maskt Ladie Night
(which blots the cloudes, the white Books of the skie)
But one sicke Phoebe, fever shaking Llight:
The heart one string: so, thus in single turnes,
The world one Phoenix, till the other burnes.

The Burning

SVppose here burnes this wonder of a breath
In righteous flames and holy heated fires:
(Like musicke which doth rapt itself to death,
Sweet'ning the inward rooms of man's desires)
So she wafts both her wings in piteous strife
Her rare dead ashes, fill a rare live urne:
One Phoenix borne another Phoenix burne.

Ignoto

The SV is emphasized in the original as it is shown above. It seems to shout Southampton and Vere as it is the only use of the 'V' to represent 'u' in the poem. And their extra size draws the reader's eye to those two letters.

Oxfordians have a wealth of material to research. We should take advantage of our authorial viewpoint to search with open minds, no matter where it leads us. There must have been important reasons to hide the Shakespeare authorship for four hundred years. Had it been a matter of 'convention', Oxford's works would have been published post-humously under his own name. There had to be serious reasons to hide him behind a pen name. Along with the obvious "non sequitur" of his not being given recognition, there is a change in his combined crown and coronet signature after Queen Elizabeth's death. The earlier signature, used from 1569 until Queen Elizabeth's death, is a picture of a crown and the top part includes an earl's coronet. Thus Oxford was making a visual double entendre, but because the signature is visual, it is also a Renaissance impresa.

After Queen Elizabeth's death, Oxford for some reason stopped using this signature, but devised a new impresa that also carried a message in the shape of a trefoil below his name. The significance of the three loops representing the Queen, Oxford and Southampton evidently escaped detection by the authorities.

1 *All The Queen's Men: Elizabeth I And Her Courtiers*; Neville Williams, p.40

2 *Acts Privy Council, 1576-1580,* pp 396-8

3 *The Biography of The Third Earl Of Southampton*; Charlotte Stopes, p.9

4 *The Biography of The Third Earl Of Southampton*; Charlotte Stopes, p.12

5 Original spelling and capitalization, except for the old style 's' resembling 'f' and 'u' as 'v'.

6 Others referred to the queen as 'Beauty'; see Raleigh's dedicatory poem in Spenser's *Faerie Queene* introduction.

APPENDIX C ✇The Persian Costume Mystery Portrait

The Persian Costume Mystery Portrait was on display at Hampton Court for nearly 200 years identified as *Elizabeth in Phantastik Habit*. Then in 1921 the label was changed to *Unknown Lady in Persian Costume*. Since then historians and iconographic specialists have been debating the identity of the 'Mysterious Lady in Persian Costume'. The real mystery may not be who the 'Unknown Lady' is, but why the identification was changed.

Iconographic specialist, Roy Strong, of the Victoria and Albert Museum, now claims that the woman is Frances Walsingham Devereux, countess of Essex. Roy Strong also mentions that it was George Vertue who originally gave the portrait its title in the first half of the 18th century. It is surely more than a coincidence that Vertue was working for, or with, Robert Harley in a multi-faceted project in 1725.

Robert Harley had married Sir Horace Vere's granddaughter and soon after was created the first earl of Oxford of the Second Creation. Several other things happened at this time. Harley and his aide, George Vertue, arranged to have the Shakespeare Memorial in Stratford 'refurbished', as well as having the statue of 'Shakespeare' installed in Westminster Abbey*. At the same time, they deposited what are now known as the Harleian Manuscripts in the British Museum. When these three things were accomplished, they threw 'the party of the century' in London to celebrate.

It is possible, even very likely, that the Persian Lady portrait was placed in Hampton Court at this time and labeled by Harley and Vertue, according to information that came with the painting from Horace Vere. It seems that Harley, when he married Horace Vere's granddaughter, acquired all of Horace Vere's papers and other items which Edward de Vere had entrusted to Horace. When Oxford went to the Continent in 1575, he made a will leaving all his possessions to Horace Vere in the event that Oxford should die on his journey. Therefore, it is more than likely that the Persian Lady portrait came into Robert Harley's hands at the same time that he acquired Sir Horace Vere's other possessions. As noted above, Roy Strong says it was Vertue who gave the Persian Lady portrait its title. It all seems to fit the sequence of events that occurred when Harley settled Sir Horace Vere's estate.

Though Roy Strong claims the portrait is the countess of Essex, he may be conforming to political pressure. Strong agrees that the artist is Gheerhaerts the younger. Then he notes that, "The face of the lady in the Persian Lady painting is very like a portrait of Queen Elizabeth hanging on the opposite wall at Hampton Court as well as several other portraits of Elizabeth by the same artist." Why does he then deny it is Queen Elizabeth and why does he set the time of its painting in the 1590's?

The late duke of Portland had in his possession at Welbeck Abbey in 1958 a portrait of Queen Elizabeth painted by Ghearhaerts the younger. At this time Elizabeth Jenkins received permission from the duke of Portland to use the portrait in her book, *Elizabeth The Great*. This portrait, labeled *Queen Elizabeth In The Garden at Wanstead 1578*, bears a striking resemblance to the Persian Lady portrait. This seems to negate Roy Strong's claim that the similar portrait of "The Persian Lady" is dated in the 1590s to 1600s.

Strong also adds, "Most of the portraits of this era by

Gheerhaerts relate to the circles of Sir Henry Lee and the earl of Essex." Strong seems to be forcing the time issue to eliminate Queen Elizabeth as the subject since she would have looked quite different in the 1590's. Yet he brings our attention to the similarity of the younger Queen Elizabeth's portrait to the Persian Lady portrait, both painted by Gheerhaerts. Might he have had a purpose in creating a misleading theory if it is still politically hot?

Next we are told the theme of the painting is the grief of the stag for an unnamed injustice he has suffered, and the compassion of the pregnant lady. The weeping stag theme is from Ovid's *Metamorphoses* in which Prince Actaeon hunting in the forest with his hounds, suddenly comes upon Diana naked in a woodland pool. Offended by being seen naked, she transforms Actaeon into a stag; his hounds then pursue him and kill him.

Strong says the woman seems to be protecting the weeping stag and putting a crown on his head. The portrait and the Sonnet in the cartouche seem to be a plea to Diana from the stag who was a prince before his transformation. Could the crown of pansies be the little purple flowers of MSND? Bottom's *anagnorisis,* or recognition, when awakened from his dream is akin to the stag's, but different because the latter must remain a stag. Yet he has a recognition of reality and can only weep for what he might have been as Prince Actaeon. A similar loss is expressed in Sonnet 87: "In sleep a king, but waking no such matter." And Sonnet 33 speaks of the loss of his son: " But out, alack, he was but one hour mine / The region (Regina) cloud has masked him from me now." The Portrait Sonnet:

> The restless swallow fits my restless mind,
> In still reviving still-renewing wrongs;
> Her just complaints of cruelty unkind

Are all the music that my life prolongs.
When pensive thoughts my weeping stag I crown,
Whose melancholy tears my cares express;
His tears in silence, and my sighs unknown,
Are all my physic that my harms redress.
My only hope was in this goodly tree,
Which I did plant in love, bring up with care;
But all in vain, for now too late I see
The shells be mine, the kernels others' are.
    My music may be plaints, my physic tears,
    If this be all the fruit my love tree bears.

Could this be Sonnet 155?

* N.B. The statue of 'Shakespeare' in Westminster Abbey stands in the *Apollo Loxias* pose. Leslie Hotson in *Shakespeare By Hilliard* says this pose with an awkward cross-legged stance, obliging the subject to lean on some sort of support, represents Apollo, "the riddling, fiddling god who speaks in riddles and tells lies." The crossed legs serve the same purpose as crossing one's fingers and telling a lie. Therefore, the statue of 'Shakespeare' in Westminster Abbey for nearly three centuries has been shouting, "I am a lie!"

❧ NOTES

Chapter One
SUMMER'S WELCOME

1 *The Queens and The Hive,* Edith Sitwell, p. 89.

2 *This Star of England,* Dorothy and Charlton Ogburn, p. 834.

3 *A Hundred Sundry Flowers;* Modern reprint of original 1573 version, additional commentary by B. Ward and Ruth Loyd Miller, available from Minos Publishing Company, P.O. Bin 1309, Jennings, LA.

4 Shakespeare's Sonnets; Edited by Israel Golanz, Introduction. 1898.

5 *This Star of England;* Dorothy and Charlton Ogburn, cit. Kittle; George Gascoigne, *A Collection of State Papers, 1571-96,* (Wm. Murdon, 1796) p.775.

6 Op.Cit. Ogburn, p. 837.

7 *The Marvelous Chance;* Father Francis Edwards, S.J., Vatican Archivist.

8 *The Armada;* Garrett Mattingly, p. 81.

9 See the essay *The Darling Buds of May* in the Appendix; Elisabeth Sears, 1996.

10 *Burke's Landed Gentry,* 18th Edition, Volume 1, p. 220, 221.

Chapter Two
FAIR FRIEND

1 *Shakespeare and The Earl of Southampton,* by G.P.V. Akrigg, p. 13.
2 Op. Cit., G.P.V. Akrigg, p. 13.
3 Akrigg, p. 13.
4 Akrigg, p. 13.
5 Akrigg, p. 13.
6 Op. Cit., Akrigg, p. 15.
7 Akrigg, p. 15.
8 Op. Cit., Akrigg, p. 16.
9 Op. Cit. Akrigg, p. 17.

Chapter Three
BEGINS A JOURNEY

1 A comment made by the Queen's half brother, Sir John Perrot.
2 *Woman's Changeableness,* poem signed 'Edward Oxenford'; *Shakespeare Identified as Edward de Vere, 17th Earl of Oxford,* by J. Thomas Looney, ed. Ruth Loyd Miller, p. 595.
3 *This Star of England,* D. & C. Ogburn, p. 93.
4 *History & Topography of the County of Essex;* cit. Ogburn, *This Star of England,* p. 78.
5 Ogburn, C. & D., p. 91.
6 *This Star of England,* D. & C. Ogburn, p.92 cit. Landsdowner mss., 19.83
7 *The Seventeenth Earl of Oxford,* Captain B. M. Ward.
8 Ophelia is Greek for "help" or "source of gain," (which aptly describes Anne as the means of Burghley's social and financial advancement). *Shakespeare: The Man Behind The Name,* Dorothy and Charlton Ogburn, Jr.

Chapter Four
MAD IN PURSUIT

1 Op. Cit. D. and C. Ogburn, p. 72.

2 *The Private Character of Queen Elizabeth,* Frederick Chamberlin; pp. 181-2; cit. Harleian mss 787, fol. 88.

3 Chamberlin, p. 182.

4 Chamberlin, p. 182.

5 There are four Sonnets of praise (127, 130, 131, and 132), eleven sonnets of pleading (135, 136, 137, 139, 140, 141, 143, 147, 149, 150, 151), three sonnets of anguished regret (119, 121, 129), and several sonnets addressed to the Queen begging forgiveness, but pointing out that she had been guilty of infidelity, too (94, 109, 110, 111, 118, 119, 142).

6 Lord Howard and Charles Arundel had made slanderous accusations of Oxford, while he, in turn, had charged them with treason. This latter charge was later proven true, for these two were involved in plots to place Mary Stuart on the throne of England. Arundel was, in fact, receiving money from Philip of Spain for this purpose. Op. Cit. Ogburn, C. & D., p. 358: Cit. Ward, B.M.: Cit Landsdowne mss., 33.6.

7 This phrase, which also appears in Sonnet 37, seems to refer to Plato's "Fable of the Cave" in which men see only shadows, but interpret them as reality.

8 Op. Cit. Ogburn, p. 359.

9 Op. Cit. Ogburn, C. & D. p. 359.

10 Op. Cit. Ogburn, p. 361: Cit. Ward, p. 224: Cit. Cal. S.P. Dom. (1581-90).

11 Op. Cit., Ogburn, C. & D., P. 362: Cit. Ward, P. 226: Cit. Landsdowne mss 104.63.

12 Ogburn, C. & D., p. 363, 365 Cit. Ward, p. 227 Cit. Lansdowne mss., 104.64.

13 Ogburn, p. 372: Ward: quot. Cotton mss., Appendix 47.

14 Birch: *Memoirs of the Reign of Q. Eliz*; p. 22.

15 Sonnet 66.

16 "Pondus" was one of the nicknames given Burghley at Court.

17 Op. Cit., C. & D. Ogburn, p. 382: cit., Ward, p. 233: Cit. Cal. Rutland mss.

Chapter Five
OUTWARD HONORING

1 *This Star of England*, D. & C. Ogburn, p. 425.

2 Ibid.

3 *The Mysterious William Shakespeare*, Charlton Ogburn, Jr., p. 688.

4 *The Seventeenth Earl of Oxford*, B.M. Ward, p. 257.

5 *The Seventeenth Earl of Oxford*, B.M. Ward, p. 293.

6 The ballad was first printed in Life's Little Day, pp. 277-281, by A.M.W. Stirling

7 *This Star of England*, D. & C. Ogburn, p. 779.

8 *The Seventeenth Earl of Oxford*, B.M. Ward, pp. 294-295.

9 "Pudder" means turmoil, pother.

Chapter Six
BEAUTY'S ROSE

1 Op. Cit. Akrigg, G.P.V., p. 35: cit. *The Progresses and Public Processions of Queen Elizabeth, Vol. II*, John Nichols, London (1788-1821).

2 *This Star of England*, D. &C. Ogburn, p.781.

Chapter Seven
FAIR LEAVES SPREAD

1 Op. Cit., Akrigg, G.V.P., p. 36: Cit. *Apollinus et Musarum Eutika Eidyllia* (Oxford, 1952) reprinted by Charles Plummer in *Elizabethan Oxford* published by the Oxford Historical Society, Vol. VIII, p. 294.
2 Op. Cit. Ogburn, C. & D., p. 854.
3 Op. Cit., Akrigg, G.V.P., p. 48: Cit. H.M.C., DeL'Isle MSS II 176.
4 Op. Cit., Akrigg, G.V.P., p. 48.
5 Op. Cit., Akrigg, G.V.P., p. 49, Cit: Collins I, P. 348.
6 Op. Cit., Akrigg, G.V.P., p. 65.
7 Op. Cit., Akrigg, G.V.P.: Cit. *Journals of The House of Lords II*, 192 ff.
8 Op. Cit. Akrigg, p. 87: Cit. Collins, II.
9 Op. Cit. Akrigg,: Cit. Stowe Ms, 167,f. 40f.
10 Op. Cit. Akrigg,: Cit. Stowe Ms, 167,f. 40f.
11 Op. Cit. Akrigg,: Cit. Cal. S.P. 12/268/50.

Chapter Eight
EDGE OF DOOM

1 Op. Cit., Akrigg, p. 77: Cit. Salisbury MSS, XIV, 197.
2 Akrigg, p. 77.
3 Ibid.
4 Akrigg, p. 80.
5 Op. Cit. Akrigg, p. 87.
6 Op. Cit., Akrigg, p. 78: Cit. W.B. Devereux, *Lives and Letters of the Devereux, Earls of Essex*, London, 1853, II, 45.
7 Op. Cit., Akrigg, p. 87.
8 Op. Cit., Akrigg, p. 89.
9 Op. Cit., Akrigg, p. 89.
10 Op. Cit., Akrigg, p. 90.
11 Op. Cit., Akrigg, p. 90.
12 Op. Cit. Akrigg, p. 92.

13 Op. Cit., Akrigg, p. 94.

14 Op. Cit., Akrigg: Cit. Collins II, 127.

15 Op. Cit., Akrigg, p. 95.

16 Op. Cit., Akrigg, p. 97.

17 Op. Cit., Akrigg: Cit. *Honors Fame in Triumph Riding*, sigs. B2v and B3r.

18 Akrigg, p. 97.

19 *The Queens and the Hive*, Dame Edith Sitwell, p. 133-139.

20 Op. Cit., Akrigg: Cit. Stopes, pp. 183-4 (also P. 170).

21 Op. Cit., Akrigg: Cit. Collins II, 216.

22 Op. Cit., Akrigg, p. 106.

23 Op. Cit., Akrigg, Cit: Bacon's Letters.

24 Op. Cit., Akrigg: Cit: Nugas Antiquae I, 179.

25 Op. Cit., Akrigg: Cit. Add. Ms. 31022 printed by Helen Georgia Stafford in *James VI of Scotland and The Throne of England* (NY, 1940), p. 215.

26 Akrigg: Cit. Add. Ms. 31022, James VI, p. 215.

27 Op. Cit., Akrigg, p. 110.

28 Op. Cit., Akrigg. p. 112.

29 Op. Cit., Akrigg: Cit. Cal. St.P. (Dom), 1598-1601, p. 580.

30 Op. Cit., Akrigg, p. 113.

31 Op. Cit., Akrigg, p. 113.

32 Op. Cit., Akrigg: Cal. St. Papers (Domestic), 1598-1601, p. 551.

33 Akrigg, p. 113.

34 Akrigg, p. 113.

35 Op. Cit., Akrigg, p. 114.

36 Op. Cit., Akrigg, p. 115.

37 Op. Cit., Akrigg, p. 115.

38 *The Gunpowder Plot*, by Hugh Ross Williamson, in *Historical Enigmas*, London 1974.

39 Op. Cit., Akrigg, p. 116.

40 Op. Cit., Akrigg: Cit. Salisbury MSS. XI, 59-61.

41 Charlotte Stopes, *The Biography of Henry Wriothesley, Third Earl of Southampton*, p. 193.

42 Charles Lord Howard of Effingham was given the additional title earl of Northampton, after his successful raid on Cadiz, where he was co-commander with Essex of the expedition.

43 Op. Cit., Akrigg: Cit. Cecil Papers, 183/121; Salisbury MSS XI, 35.

44 Op. Cit., Akrigg: Cit. *Elizabethan England*, SI, 432.

45 Op. Cit., Akrigg, p. 120. Thomas Lee, who had served Essex well in Ireland, was the nephew of Sir Henry Lee, the long-time promoter and organizer of the Queen's birthday jousting tournaments, as well as a champion in those tournaments, but who was defeated by Oxford in his debut performance in 1572. Anne Vavasour lived with Sir Henry Lee from 1589 until his death and bore him a son, Thomas, possibly the same Thomas referred to in the account above as his nephew.

46 Akrigg, p. 120.

47 Op. Cit., Akrigg, p. 120.

48 Op. Cit., Akrigg: Cit. Acts P.C., 1600-1601, p. 150.

49 Op. Cit., Akrigg, p. 121.

50 Op. Cit., Akrigg: Cit. S.P. 12/278, f. 188r (public Record Office).

51 Op. Cit., Akrigg: Cit. Jardine, David., *Criminal Trials* (London 1847) I, 321.

52 Op. Cit., Akrigg, p. 123.

53 *All the Queen's Men*, Neville Williams, p. 239.

54 Op. Cit., Akrigg, p. 123.

55 Op. Cit., Akrigg: Cit. S.P. 12/278, f. 198r.

56 Op. Cit., Akrigg: Cit. Jardine, I, 363-365.

57 Op. Cit., Akrigg: Cit. Letter from R. Cecil to Charles Blount, earl of Mountjoy in Ireland. Cal. S.P. (Dom), 1598-1601, p. 598.

58 Op. Cit., Akrigg: Cit. Examination of February 16th, Cal. S.P. (Dom) 1598-1601, p. 571.

59 Op. Cit., Akrigg, p. 127.

Chapter Nine
BARE RUINED CHOIRS

1 Akrigg, p. 130.
2 Akrigg, p. 130.
3 *The Gunpowder Plot*, from *Enigmas in History*, by Hugh Ross Williamson.
4 *All the Queen's Men*, Neville Williams; p. 244.
5 Neville Williams, p. 244.
6 Op. Cit., Neville Williams, p. 245.
7 Op. Cit., Williams, p. 246 (An echo of Oxford's phrase in his letter to Burghley, p. 44 and Sonnet 37, p. 53).
8 Ibid.
9 *All The Queen's Men*, Neville Williams, p. 247.
10 *All The Queen's Men*, Williams. p. 247.
11 *The Life and Times of General Sir Edward Cecil*, Charles Dalton, F.R.G.S, Volume 1, p. 209.
12 *All The Queen's Men*, Williams, p. 248.
13 *The Sayings of Queen Elizabeth*, Frederick Chamberlain, p. 310.
14 *All The Queen's Men*, Neville Williamson, p. 260.
15 Ibid.
16 *This Star of England*, C. & D. Ogburn, p. 1182.
17 Op. Cit. C. & D. Ogburn, p. 1190.
18 Op. Cit. C. & D. Ogburn, p. 1190.
19 Op. Cit., C. & D. Ogburn, p. 1201.
20 Discontented nobles fled to France in Richard II's reign, then with an army and Richard's exiled cousin to lead them, they returned, defeated Richard, and proclaimed Bolingbroke Henry IV.
21 Southampton in the tower.
22 Op. Cit., C. & D. Ogburn, p. 923.
23 Op. Cit., Akrigg, p. 141.
24 Op. Cit., Akrigg, p. 141.
25 Op. Cit. C. & D. Ogburn, p. 1202.

Chapter Ten
DREAMING ON THINGS TO COME

1 Akrigg, Cit. *The Oglander Memoirs* (London, 1888), p. 23.
2 Akrigg. Cit. W. p. 122.
3 Akrigg, p. 136, Cit. W. P. 122.
4 Akrigg, p. 145.
5 Akrigg, p. 153, Cit. Salisbury MSS., XVIII, 304.
6 Akrigg, Ibid.
7 Akrigg, p. 155.
8 Akrigg, p. 156, Cit. *The Life and Reign of James* in Kennet's *Complete History*, II, 736.
9 Akrigg, p. 157.
10 Akrigg, p. 157.
11 Akrigg, p. 157.
12 Akrigg, p. 157, Footnote.
13 Akrigg, p. 157.
14 Akrigg, p. 158.
15 Akrigg, p. 163.
16 Akrigg, p. 164.
17 Akrigg, p. 165.
18 Akrigg, p. 165.
19 Akrigg, p. 166.
20 Akrigg, p. 171.
21 Akrigg, p. 171.
22 Akrigg, p. 172.
23 Akrigg, p. 172.
24 Akrigg, p. 173
25 Akrigg, p. 174, Cit. *The Life and Reign of James the First* in *A Complete History*, II, 789.
26 Akrigg, p. 174, foot note #3.

† BIBLIOGRAPHY

Adlington, William (sic; pseudonymous/Vere?) Trans. *The Golden Ass of Lucius Apuleius*, ed. F. J. Harvey Darton. Hogarth Press, New York.

Akrigg, G. V. P. *Shakespeare and the Earl of Southampton*. Harvard University Press, Cambridge, MA, 1968.

Alpers, Paul J., ed. *Elizabethan Poetry; Modern Essays in Criticism*. Oxford University Press, Oxford, England, 1967.

Anonymous (sic; Edward de Vere). *Richard The Second or Thomas of Woodstock*. Malone Society Reprint, Oxford University Reprint, 1929.

Anthony, Katherine. *Queen Elizabeth*. Alfred Knopf, N.Y., 1929.

Appleton, Elizabeth. *Edward De Vere and the War of Words*. Elizabethan Press, Toronto, 1985.

Ashley, Robert and Moseley, Edwin M., intro. and notes by. *Elizabethan Fiction*. Rhinehart & Co., Inc., N.Y., 1953.

Axton, Marie, ed. *Three Tudor Classic Interludes*. D.S. Brewer, Cambridge, England. Rowan & Littlefield, Totowa, N.J., 1982.

Baade, Eric C., Seneca's *Tragedies; Oedipus; Troas; Agamemnon*. MacMillan, London, 1969.

Baker, Howard, *Elizabethan Poetry, Formation of the Heroic Medium*.

Bald, R. C., ed. *Six Elizabethan Plays*. Riverside Editions, Houghton Mifflin Co., Boston, 1963.

Barbour, C. L. *Shakespeare's Festive Comedy*. Princeton University Press, Princeton, N.J., 1959.

Beckerman, Bernard. *Shakespeare at the Globe, 1599-1609*. Collier-MacMillan Ltd., London, 1962.

Bender, Robert M., ed. *Five Courtier Poets of the English Renaissance*. Washington Square Press, N.Y., 1969.

Bentley, Richard. *Elizabethan Whodunit—Who Was "William Shakespeare?"* American Bar Association Journal, Feb. 1959, Vol. 45.

Bindoff, S. T. *Tudor England.* Penguin Books, Harmondsworth, Middlesex, England, 1950.

Boas, Frederick S. *An Introduction To Tudor Drama.* Oxford University Press, London, 1959.

Boas, Frederick S. *Works of Thomas Kyd.* Clarendon Press, Oxford, 1901.

Boccaccio, Giovanni. *The Decameron.* Trans. by John Payne. Modern Library Edition, New York.

Bond, R. Warwick, M. A. *The Complete Works of John Lyly,* Vol. I-III. Oxford, 1902.

Booth, Stephen. *An Essay on Shakespeare's Sonnets.* Yale University Press, 1969.

Boroff, Edith. *Music in Europe and the United States: A History.* Prentice-Hall, Inc., Englewood Cliffs, N.J., 1971.

Bowen, Catherine Drinker. *Francis Bacon; The Temper of a Man.* An Atlantic Monthly Press Book. Little Brown & Co. Boston, 1963.

Bowers, Fredson Thayer. *Elizabethan Revenge Tragedy, 1587-1642.* Peter Smith, Gloucester, MA, 1959.

Braden, Gordon. *The Classics and English Renaissance Poetry.* Yale University Press, New Haven and London, 1978.

Brown, Charles Armitage. *Shakespeare's Autobiographical Poems.* James, Bohn, West Strand, London, 1838.

Bullough, Geoffrey. *Narrative and Dramatic Sources of Shakespeare. Vols. I-VIII.* Columbia University Press, N.Y., 1951.

Burgess, Anthony. *Shakespeare.* Alfred Knopf, N.Y., 1970.

Bush, Douglas. *The Renaissance and English Humanism.* University of Toronto Press, 1939.

Cable, Mary and Editors of Newsweek Book Division. *El Escorial.* Newsweek, New York, 1971.

Calderwood, James J. and Tolliver, Harold E., eds. *Essays in Shakespearean Criticism*. Prentice-Hall, Englewood Cliffs, N.J., 1970.

Campbell, Lily B. *Shakespeare's Histories, Mirrors of Elizabethan Policy*. J. W. Arrowsmith Ltd., Bristol, England, 1980.

Campbell, Lily B. *Shakespeare's Tragic Heroes: Slaves of Passion*. Reprint Barnes & Noble, by spec. arr. Cambridge Univ. Press, 1959.

Cardano, Girolamo. *Cardanus' Comfort*, 1576. Da Capo Press Reprint, New York, 1969.

Cassirer, Ernst; Kristeller, Paul O.; Randall, John H., eds. *The Renaissance Philosophy of Man*. University of Chicago Press, 1948.

Chapman, Hester. *Two Tudor Portraits: Henry Howard, Earl of Surrey and Lady Katherine Grey*. Little, Brown and Company, Boston, 1960.

Clark, Eva Turner. *Hidden Allusions in Shakespeare's Plays*. Williams Farquhar Payson, N.Y. 1931. Minos Publishing Co. Jennings, LA, 1974.

Chamberlin, Frederick. *The Private Character of Queen Elizabeth*. Dodd, Mead & Co., N.Y., 1922.

Chute, Marchette. *Geoffrey Chaucer of England*. E. P. Dutton & Co., Inc., New York, 1946.

Chute, Marchette. *Shakespeare of London*. E. P. Dutton and Company, Inc. New York, 1949.

Clemen, Wolfgang H. *The Development of Shakespeare's Imagery*. Harvard University Press, Cambridge, MA, 1962.

Costain, Thomas B. *The Three Edwards*. Doubleday and Company, Inc. Garden City, N.Y., 1958.

Costain, Thomas B. *The Last Plantagenets*. Doubleday and Company, Inc. Garden City, N.Y., 1962.

Cunningham, J. V. *The Renaissance in England*. Harcourt, Brace & World, N.Y., 1966.

Dalton, Charles, F.R.G.S *The Life and Times of General Sir Edward Cecil*. London: Sampson, Low, Marston, Searle & Rivingston, 1885

Dart, Thurston. *Foreword to A Plain and Easy Introduction to Practical Music*, by Thomas Morley. R. Alec Harman, ed. Norton, N.Y. 1953.

Dean, Leonard, ed. *Shakespeare: Modern Essays in Criticism*. Oxford University Press, New York, 1967.

Dodd, A. H. *Life in Elizabethan England*. Capricorn Books, G. P. Putnam's Sons. Reprint permission, B. T. Batsford, Ltd., 1961.

Dowden, Edward. I. *Shakspeare: A Critical Study of His Mind And Art*. Harper & Brothers, New York.

Economou, George D., ed. *Geoffrey Chaucer: A Collection of Original Articles*. McGraw-Hill Book Company, New York, 1975.

Eliot, T. S. *Essays on Elizabethan Drama*. Harcourt, Brace & World, N.Y., 1932.

_____. "Hamlet and His Problems," in *Twentieth Century Interpretations of Hamlet*, ed. David Bevington. Prentice-Hall, Englewood, N.J., 1968.

_____. *Selected Essays*. Faber and Faber, Ltd., London, 1932.

Ellis-Fermor, Una. *Some Recent Research In Shakespeare's Imagery*. Publ. For Shakespeare Assoc. by Oxford University Press, London, 1937.

Elson, Louis C. *Shakespeare in Music*. Boston, 1901.

Emerson, Ralph Waldo. *Representative Men: Shakespeare The Poet*.

England, Martha Winburn. *Garrick and Stratford*. New York Public Library, New York, 1962.

Erickson, Carolly. *The First Elizabeth*. Summit Books, N.Y., 1983.

_____. *Mistress Anne: The Exceptional Life of Anne Boleyn*. Summit Books, N.Y., 1984.

Erskine, John. *The Elizabethan Lyric*. Columbia University Press, N.Y., 1903

Fluchere, Henri. *Shakespeare and the Elizabethans*. Guy Hamilton, trans. Hill and Wang, N.Y., 1956.

Fowler, William Plumer. *Shakespeare's Phoenix and the Turtle. An*

Interpretation: Supplementary Exegisis by Dorothy Ogburn. Peter Randall, Portsmouth, N.H., 1986.

Fowler, William Plumer. *Shakespeare Revealed in Oxford's Letters*. Peter Randall, Portsmouth, N.H., 1986.

Fox, J. A. *A Time Scheme For Shakespeare's Sonnets*. The Mitre Press, London, 1929.

Fraser, Antonia. *Mary Queen of Scots*. Delacorte Press, New York, 1970.

Fraser, Russell A.; Rabkin, Norman, eds. *Drama of the English Renaissance, Vol. I, The Tudor Period*. Macmillan Publishing Co., N.Y., 1976.

French, Peter J. *John Dee: The World of an Elizabethan Magus*. Routledge and Kegan Paul, London, 1972.

Frey, David L. *The First Tetralogy, Shakespeare's Scrutiny of The Tudor Myth*. Moutin, The Hague & Paris, 1976.

Fripp, Edgar I. *Shakespeare Studies, Biographical and Literary*. Oxford University Press, London, 1930.

Froissart, Sir John. *Chronicles of England, France and Spain, Vol. I & II*. Thomas Johnes, trans. Colonial Press, London & N.Y., 1901.,

Giamatti, A. Bartlett. *The Earthly Paradise and the Renaissance Epic*. Princeton University Press, 1966.

Gillingham, John. *The Wars Of the Roses; Peace and Conflict in Fifteenth-Century England*. Louisiana State University Press, Baton Rouge, 1981.

Giroux, Robert. *The Book Known as Q: A Consideration of Shakespeare's Sonnets*. Vintage Books Division of Random House, N.Y., 1983.

Goddard, Harold C. *Alphabet of the Imagination*. Eds., Eleanor Goddard Worthen and Margaret Goddard Holt. Humanities Press, N.J., 1974.

—————————. *The Meaning of Shakespeare, Vol. I & II*. Phoenix Books, University of Chicago Press, Chicago & London, 1968.

Gohn, Jack Benoit. *Richard II: Shakespeare's Legal Brief On the Royal*

Prerogative and the Succession to the Throne. Georgetown Law Journal, Vol. 70, Number 3, Feb. 1982.

Golding, Louis Thorn. *An Elizabethan Puritan: Life of Arthur Golding*. Richard R. Smith, N.Y. 1937.

Goodfellow, Peter. *Shakespeare's Birds*. Kestrel Books, Penguin Books, Ltd., Hammondsworth, Middlesex, England, 1983.

Gottfried Rudolf, ed. *Ariosto's Orlando Furioso*. Selections from the translation of Sir John Harington. Indiana University Press, 1971.

Granville-Barker, Harley. *Prefaces To Shakespeare*. B. T. Batsford Ltd., London, 1930, Third Impression, 1977.

Greenwood, Sir George. *The Shakespeare Problem Restated*. Greenwood Press, Westport, Conn., 1970. Orig. pub., Bodley Head, London, 1908.

Gurr, Andrew. *The Shakespeare Stage, 1574-1642*. Cambridge University Press, 1970.

Hallam, Elizabeth, ed. *The Plantagenet Chronicles*. Weidenfeld & Nicolson, New York, 1986.

Harbage, Alfred, ed. *Shakespeare, The Tragedies: A Collection of Critical Essays*. Prentice Hall, Englewood Cliffs, N.J., 1964.

Harrison, G. B., ed. *The Letters of Queen Elizabeth*. Casell, London, 1935.

Harvey, John. *The Plantagenets*. Revised Edition, William Collins Sons & Co. Ltd., Glasgow, 1959.

Heilman, Robert B., ed. *An Anthology of English Drama before Shakespeare*. Holt, Rhinehart and Winston, Inc., New York, 1952.

Hexter, J. H. *Reappraisals in History*. Northwestern University Press and Longman's Green & Co. Ltd., G.B., 1961.

Hopkins, Samuel. *The Puritans; The Church, Court and Parliament of England During the Reigns of Edward VI and Queen Elizabeth, Vol. III*. Gould and Lincoln, Boston, 1861.

Hotson, Leslie. *The Death of Marlowe*.

_____. *Shakespeare by Hilliard, A Portrait Deciphered*. Univ. of California Press, Berkeley and Los Angeles, 1977.

Howarth, Herbert. *The Tiger's Heart, Eight Essays on Shakespeare*. Oxford University Press, N.Y., 1970.

Huizinga, Johan. *Erasmus and the Age of Reformation*. Harper Torch Books/The Cloister Library, Harper & Row, New York, 1957.

Huizinga, Johan. *The Waning of the Middle Ages*. Doubleday Anchor Books, Garden City, N.Y., 1954.

Hume, Martin A. S. *The Courtships of Queen Elizabeth*. MacMillan Co., N.Y., T. Fisher Unwin, London, 1896.

Irwin, Margaret. *Young Bess*. Harcourt, Brace & World, N.Y., 1945.

_____. *Elizabeth, Captive Princess*. Harcourt, Brace & Co., 1948.

_____. *That Great Lucifer*. Harcourt, Brace and Company, New York, 1960.

Javitch, Daniel. *Poetry and Courtliness in Renaissance England*. Princeton University Press, 1978.

Jenkins, Elizabeth. *Elizabeth the Great*. Capricorn Books, N.Y., 1958.

Johnson, Paul. *Elizabeth I*. Holt, Rhinehart & Winston, N.Y., 1974.

Johnston, George Burke, ed. *Poems of Ben Jonson*. Harvard University Press, Cambridge, MA, 1954.

Jonson, Ben. *Bartholomew Fair*. A. B. Kernan & R. B. Young, eds. Yale University Press, New Haven, CN., 1963.

Jonson, Ben. *Every Man In His Humor*. A. B. Kernan & R. B. Young, eds. Yale University Press, New Haven, CN., 1969.

Kaufmann, Ralph J., ed. *Elizabethan Drama*; Modern Essays in Criticism. A Galaxy Book, Oxford University Press, New York, 1961.

Kelly, Amy. *Eleanor of Aquitaine and the Four Kings*. Harvard University Press, Cambridge, 1950.

Ker, W. P. *Medieval English Literature*. Oxford University Press, London, Oxford, New York, 1912. Reprint 1969.

Kirsch, James. *Shakespeare's Royal Self*. G. P. Putnam's Son, N.Y., 1966.

Kittredge, George Lyman, & Ribner, Irving, eds. *The Complete Works of Shakespeare*. Ginn and Co., Waltham, MA 1971.

Kristeller, Paul Oskar. *Renaissance Thought and its Sources*. Columbia University Press, N.Y., 1979.

Kökeritz, Helge. *Mr. William Shakespeare's Comedies, Histories, & Tragedies: A Facsimile Edition*. Yale University Press, New Haven, 1954.

Lamb, Margaret. *Beyond Revenge: The Spanish Tragedy*. From Mosaic, Vol. IX, no. 1, A Journal For the Comparative Study of Literature and Ideas. University of Manitoba Press, 1975.

Lambin, Georges. *Voyages de Shakespeare en France et en Italie*. Librairie E. Droz, Geneve, 1962.

Latham, Agnes, ed. *Poems of Sir Walter Raleigh*. Harvard University Press, Cambridge, MA, 1962.

Lawlis, Merritt, ed. *Elizabethan Prose Fiction*. The Odyssey Press, Bobbs-Merrill Co., Inc., Indianapolis & N.Y., 1967.

Lee, Sir Sidney. *A Life of William Shakespeare*. The MacMillan Company, New York, 1908.

Leishman, J. B. *Themes and Variations in Shakespeare's Sonnets*. Harper Torchbooks, Harper & Row, New York, 1961, 1963, 1966.

Levin, Harry. *The Question of Hamlet*. Viking Press, N.Y., 1961. Orig. pub. Oxford University Press, 1959.

Levin, Harry. *The Over-reacher*. Harvard University Press, Cambridge, MA.

Lofts, Norah. *Anne Boleyn*. Coward, McCann & Geoghegan, Inc., N.Y., 1979.

Long, John H. *Shakespeare's Use of Music; A Study of the Music and its Performance in the Original Production of Seven Comedies*. Da Capo Press, N.Y., 1977. Originally published by University of Florida, 1955.

Long, John H. *Shakespeare's Use of Music: The Final Comedies*. Da Capo

Press, New York, 1977. Published by University of Florida, 1961.

Looney, J. Thomas. *Shakespeare Identified in Edward de Vere, The Seventeenth Earl of Oxford.* Duell, Sloan and Pearce, New York, 1920.

Looney, J. Thomas. *The Poems Of Edward de Vere.* London, 1921.

Luke, Mary N. *A Crown For Elizabeth.* Coward-McCann, New York, 1970.

Luke, Mary N. *Gloriana: The Years of Elizabeth I.* Coward-McCann, New York, 1973.

MacDonald, Hugh, ed. *England's Helicon.* Harvard University Press, Cambridge, 1962.

Mack, Maynard. *World Masterpieces, Vol. I: Literature of Western Culture through the Renaissance.* W. W. Norton & Co., Inc., New York, 1973.

Madden, Right Hon. D. H., Vice Chancellor, University of Dublin. *The Diary of Master William Silence: A Study of Shakespeare and Elizabethan Sport.* Longmans, Green, and Co., London, New York, & Bombay, 1897.

Marder, Louis. *His Exits and His Entrances: The Story of Shakespeare's Reputation.* J. B. Lippincott Company, Philadelphia and New York, 1963.

May, Stephen W. *The Poems of Edward de Vere, Seventeenth Earl of Oxford and of Robert Devereux, Second Earl of Essex.* Studies in Philology, Vol. LXXVII, No. 5. University of North Carolina Press, 1980.

Mattingly, Garrett. *The Armada.* Houghton Mifflin Company, Boston, 1959.

McFee, William. *Sir Martin Frobisher.* John Lane, The Bodley Head Ltd., London, 1928.

Miller, Ruth Lloyd, ed. *Shakespeare Identified*, by J. Thomas Looney, Vol. I & II. Minos Publishing Company, Jennings, LA 1975.

_____.*The Crown Signature: An Enigma Awaiting Time's Solution.* (c) Ms. 1988.

Milligan, Burton A., ed. *Three Renaissance Classics, The Prince, Utopia, The Courtier*. Charles Scribners & Sons, New York, 1953.

Moncur, A. H. *Shakespeare: His Music and Song*. Kegan Paul, Trench, Trubner & Co., Ltd. London (no date).

Morgan, Appleton. *A Study in The Warwickshire Dialect*. The Shakespeare Press, Shakespeare Society of New York, N.Y., 1899.

Muir, Kenneth and S. Schoenbaum. *A New Companion To Shakespeare Studies*. Cambridge University Press, Cambridge, 5th Reprint, 1979.

Naylor, Edward W. *Shakespeare and Music*. Da Capo Press and Benjamin Blom, Inc., New York, 1965.

Neilson, Wm. A., ed. *Chief Elizabethan Dramatists*. Houghton Mifflin, Cambridge, Mass., 1911.

Newton, Thomas, ed. *Seneca: His Ten Tragedies: Translated into English*, with introduction by T. S. Eliot. AMS Press, N.Y., 1967.

Nims, J. Frederick, ed. *Ovid's Metamorphoses: The Arthur Golding (sic) Translation (1567)*. McMillan, N.Y., 1965.

Noble, Richmond. *Shakespeare's Use of Song (With the Text of the Principle Songs)*. Oxford University Press, London, 1923.

Norman, Charles. *The Muses' Darling: The Life of Christopher Marlowe*. Rhinehart and Co., New York, 1946.

Nulle, Stebelton H., *Classics Of Western Thought: Vol. I, the Ancient World*. Harcourt, Brace & World, Inc., New York, 1968.

Ogburn, Charlton and Dorothy. *This Star of England*. Coward-McCann, New York, 1952.

_____. *The Renaissance Man of England*, Coward-McCann, Inc., New York.

Ogburn, Charlton, Jr. and Dorothy. *Shakespeare: The Man Behind the Name*. William Morrow & Co., New York, 1962.

Ogburn, Charlton, Jr. *The Mysterious William Shakespeare: The Myth and the Reality*. Dodd, Mead & Company, New York, 1984.

_____. *The Mystery of William Shakespeare (Foreword by Lord Vere)*.

Sphere Books Ltd., Penguin Group, London, England, 1988.

Orgel, Stephen, ed. *Christopher Marlowe: The Complete Poems and Translations*. Penguin Books Ltd., Harmondsworth, Middlesex, Eng. 1971.

Ottman, Robert W. *Elementary Harmony: Theory and Practice*. Prentice-Hall, Inc., Englewood Cliffs, N.J., 1970.

Ovid (Publius Ovidius Naso). *Metamorphoses*. Arthur Golding, trans. (sic), W. H. D. Rouse, ed. De La More Press, London, 1904.

Ovid (Publius Ovidius Naso). *Metamorphoses*. Rolfe Humphries, trans. Indiana University Press, 1955.

Packe, Michael (ed. and completed by L. C. B. Seaman). *King Edward III*. Routledge & Kegan Paul, London, 1983.

Payne, Edward John, ed. Additional notes by C. Raymond Beazley. *Voyages of the Elizabethan Seamen: Select Narratives From the Principal Navigations of Hakluyt*. Clarendon Press, Oxford, 1936.

Phillips, O. Hood. *Shakespeare and the Lawyers*. Methuen and Co., Ltd., London, England, 1972.

Pickering, John (sic; Pseudonym, Vere?). *Horestes, An Interlude of Vice*, ed. Daniel Seltzer. Malone Society Reprint, Oxford University Press, 1968.

Plutarch. *Lives of the Noble Romans*. Edmund Fuller, ed. Dell Publishing Co., Inc., New York, 1959.

Prouty, C. T. *George Gascoigne: Elizabethan Courtier, Soldier, and Poet*. Benjamin Blom, New York, 1942.

Pulman, Michael Barraclough. *The Elizabethan Privy Council in the Fifteen Seventies*. University of California Press, Berkeley, Los Angeles, London, 1971.

Purdon, Noel. *The Words of Mercury, Shakespeare and English Mythology and the Renaissance*. fr. Elizabethan and Renaissance Studies. Dr. James Hogg, ed. Salzburg Studies in English Literature, Institute für Englische Sprach und Literatur, Universitat Salzburg, Austria, 1974.

Rabkin, Norman, ed. *Approaches to Shakespeare*. McGraw-Hill, New York, 1964.

Read, Conyers. *Lord Burghley and Queen Elizabeth*. Fletcher and Son, Ltd., Norwich, 1960.

Reed, Edward Bliss, ed. *Songs from the British Drama*. Yale University Press, 1925.

Reese, M. M. *Elizabethan Verse Romances*. Routledge & Kegan Paul, London. 1968.

Rendall, Canon G. H. *Shakespeare's Sonnets and Edward de Vere*. London, 1930.

Ribner, Irving, ed. *Complete Plays of Christopher Marlowe*. Odyssey Press, Bobbs-Merrill Co., Inc., Indianapolis and New York.

Ross, Charles. *Richard III*. University of California Press, Berkeley and Los Angeles, 1981.

Saccio, Peter. *The Court Comedies of John Lyly, A Study in Allegorical Dramaturgy*. Princeton University Press, Princeton, N.J., 1969.

_____. *Shakespeare's English Kings*. Oxford University Press, New York, 1977.

Siegel, Paul N., ed. *His Infinite Variety: Major Shakespearean Criticism Since Johnson*. J. B. Lippincott Co., Philadelphia, 1964.

Siegel, Paul N. *Shakespeare In His Time And Ours*. University of Notre Dame Press, Notre Dame, Indiana, 1968.

Simpson, Claude M. *The British Broadside Ballad and Its Music*. Rutgers University Press, N.J., 1966.

Singleton, Esther. *Shakespeare's Garden*. Century Co., N.Y., 1922. Reprinted Gale Research Co., Book Tower, Detroit, 1974.

Sitwell, Dame Edith. *Fanfare For Elizabeth*. The MacMillan Company, New York, 1946.

_____. *The Queens and The Hive*. Little, Brown and Company, Boston, 1962.

Smith, Lacey Baldwin. *The Elizabethan World; Horizon Book*. American Heritage Publishing Company, New York, 1967.

Spencer, Hazelton, ed. *Elizabethan Plays*. Little, Brown and Co., Boston, MA, 1933.

Spencer, Theodore. *Shakespeare and The Nature of Man*. MacMillan Co., New York, 1942.

Stewart, Charles D. *Some Textual Difficulties In Shakespeare*. Yale University Press, New Haven, 1914.

Sylvester, Richard S., ed. *The Anchor Anthology of Sixteenth Century Verse*. Anchor Press, Doubleday, Garden City, N.Y., 1974.

Sypher, Wylie. *The Ethic Of Time*. Seabury Press, N.Y., 1970.

Traversi, Derek. *Shakespeare, The Last Phase*. Harcourt, Brace and Co., New York, 1953.

_____. *An Approach To Shakespeare*. Doubleday & Company, Inc., Garden City, N.Y., 1956.

Tucker, T. G. *The Sonnets of Shakespeare*. Cambridge University Press, Cambridge, 1924.

Tydeman, William, ed. *Four Tudor Comedies*. Penguin, New York, 1984.

Ure, Peter, ed. *King Richard II*. Arden Shakespeare, Methuen & Co. Ltd., 1978.

Vaughn, Jack A., *Shakespeare's Comedies*, Ungar Publishing Co., N.Y., 1980.

West, Robert H. *Shakespeare and The Outer Mystery*. University of Kentucky Press, 1968.

West, Robert H. *The Invisible World: A Study of Pneumatology In Elizabethan Drama*. Octagon Books, N.Y., 1969.

Walker, Ernest. *A History of Music in England*, Third Edition, revised and enlarged by J. A. Westrup. Oxford at the Clarendon Press, 1952.

Ward, Capt. Bernard M. *The Seventeenth Earl of Oxford (1550-1604) From Contemporary Documents*. John Murray, London, 1928.

Ward, Capt. Bernard M., ed. *A Hundreth Sundrie Flowers, From the Original Edition*, Frederick Etchells & Hugh Macdonald, London,